Mentoring Through Prayer

Mentoring Through Prayer

Preventing The Autopsy

REV CRAIG G WASHINGTON

ISBN: 1507686234
ISBN 13: 9781507686232

Table of Contents

Foreword

I am honored and privileged to be the friend of Craig G. Washington, a friend, a mentor, a prayer warrior, a minister of the gospel, a loving father, a wonderful husband, a philanthropist, and, most importantly, a man who loves God more than anything else on the face of this earth. As Craig's and my friendship began to strengthen, I noticed something unique about him: his ability, in the middle of chaos or a crisis, to interrupt the enemy and begin to pray! Prayer and communication with God is Craig's calling card, and it is no surprise that God trusted him in such a unique way to share with him in great detail how much of what happens in our modern church has removed us from his glory. One thing I am grateful for is that as God was calling me to "step out from among them" and answer my calling, there was something I needed at that crucial time in my life. I needed a friend that could help guide me to the road less traveled. The road where trailblazing is required. A friend who could encourage the crucifixion required to make a difference in the lives of others. A friend who was willing not only to guide me to that road but also to pack a bag and make the journey with me! Craig is that friend.

After well over twenty years of ministry and seeing all the ups and downs of spiritual man versus natural man, Craig was compelled by God to give us Christians a viable handbook on much of what happens with ministry that is literally grieving the Holy Spirit to his core! And the revelation is so profound that a highlighter must be purchased to accompany your read. This book is absolutely revolutionary and prophetic! It will change your life and save you much time in identifying ministries that need to be abandoned immediately. Like my mother used to say, some ministries we need to run from with the same intensity as if our house was on fire. As you begin to surrender everything to God and understand what he is asking of us, this book will be necessary in moving forward with God and operating outside the box of traditionalism and religiosity. There is more God is asking of us, and many of us recognize "box" ministry and the fact that God is calling us to a higher place in him than what we are experiencing. The writing has been on the wall for change, and after reading this book, there will be no doubt what your next move in God should be. This book will provide clarity to many of those struggling in the "quicksand" of carnal ministry. This book will change your life!

Rod Green
Servant Leader, Greater Works Fellowship
Servant for Christ

Prelude

Have you ever been in church and thought to yourself, "What would the perfect church look like?" Well, forget about it—it's not going to happen. At least not here on earth. Unfortunately, I've asked myself this question more than a million times. I've been saved (accepted Jesus Christ as my Lord and Savior) and attending churches for twenty-five years as a member, as a church builder, and as a part of pastoral teams; I've mentored many young leaders and pastors, worn many hats, and held many titles. After all that I've been through, I've never seen nor experienced a perfect church.

So God has given me the daunting, seemingly insurmountable assignment of helping the church (not God) to address some of its transgressions, with real, concrete solutions. You're probably saying, "Many have tried, many have succeeded, and many have failed." Here's a conundrum: I'm just being obedient to what God has asked me to do. He says in Isaiah 1:19–20, "If you are willing and obedient, you will eat the good of the things of the land, but if you resist and rebel, you will be devoured by the sword." For the mouth of the Lord has spoken.

OK, so the mouth of the Lord spoke, and I began to write. I would like to think that this assignment took on (if you will) twenty-five years of investigative hands-on reporting. I sat; I watched; I worked, taught, preached, and prophesied. However, in the already-established churches, there always seemed to be missing links/missing pieces. The Holy Spirit identified these missing links/pieces as transgressions.

So this book, Application, teaching, or even curriculum is about twelve of the transgressions that perhaps hinder the body of Christ from reaching its achievable goals. Of course, there are some churches that consider themselves to be perfect and to have it all together. This book may or may not serve them any purpose. Each transgression identified requires what God has given me to coin an approach called "mentoring through prayer".

Saul's desperate need for someone to pray for his transgressions David became his into counsel via playing the harp/lyre.

"Why the title *Mentoring through Prayer*, God?" I asked. He said, "Because many ministers and leaders are unapproachable and believe they've arrived, so you have to mentor them from a distance, in the spirit."

So buckle your seat belts and prepare for perhaps one of the most provocative journeys in your life. To whom is this book written? I would like to think it's to all of the leaders/officers of the church. However, I believe it is more of a guide/App. for the laypeople sitting and dying in the pews and how they are to pray for their leaders.

Rev. Craig G. Washington
Greater Works Fellowship

One

Then Samuel took the horn of oil and anointed him in the midst of his brothers; and the Spirit of the Lord came upon David from that day forward. So Samuel arose and went to Ramah.

But the Spirit of the Lord departed from Saul, and a distressing spirit from the Lord troubled him. And Saul's servants said to him, "Surely, a distressing spirit from God is troubling you. Let our master now command your servants, who are before you, to seek out a man who is a skillful player on the harp. And it shall be that he will play it with his hand when the distressing spirit from God is upon you, and you shall be well." So Saul said to his servants, "Provide me now a man who can play well, and bring him to me." Then one of the servants answered and said, "Look, I have seen a son of Jesse the Bethlehemite, who is skillful in playing, a mighty man of valor, a man of war, prudent in speech, and a handsome person; and the

Lord is with him." Therefore Saul sent messengers to Jesse, and said, ""Send me your son David, who is with the sheep." And Jesse took a donkey loaded with bread, a skin of wine, and a young goat, and sent them by his son David to Saul. So David came to Saul and stood before him. And he loved him greatly, and he became his armor-bearer. Then Saul sent to Jesse, saying, "Please let David stand before me, for he has found favor in my sight." And so it was, whenever the spirit from God was upon Saul, that David would take a harp/lyre and play it with his hand Then Saul would become re freshed and well, and the distressing spirit would depart from him.

The origin of this Holy Spirit–inspired book, comes from the above passage. When I was reading and studying this passage, the Holy Spirit birthed the concept in me of "Mentoring through Prayer". The Holy Spirit also brought to my remembrance how many young pastors I've mentored through prayer throughout the years. What does this all mean? Some men and women of God are approachable; some are not. So as to avoid preaching the above message, I will just say that in a matter of two verses, David was anointed future king (and the spirit of God ascended upon him) while in the very next verse the current (soon-to-be-dethroned) king was experiencing the spirit of the Lord, departing. I would submit that Saul was terrified and needed someone (NOT, just anyone) to pray/intercede for him. However, the form of prayer applied and instituted was that of playing the harp/lyre. The Holy Spirit revealed to me that prayer can take many forms—for example, playing the harp (or any instrument), singing (especially in the spirit), dancing, writing, shouting, clapping, teaching, preaching, and prophesying. Ironically, little did anyone know that the same spirit distressing Saul was the same spirit that would one day try to kill David?

David was summoned and chosen for the task.

David never opened his mouth throughout this demon-distressing, spirit-chasing session; he only played his harp. He never said mumbling a word.

"When Gods Calls and Assigns us to pray"

1. Many times, people you are assigned to will receive you better behind the scenes. In other words, you don't have to mentor them face-to-face.
2. Many times, the Holy Spirit assigns us to people to play or pray for them, and we abdicate our assignment.
3. Many times, the very people we play, sing, or pray for are the very people we may one day replace.

Distressing spirits are all around us, including within ourselves. When we become instruments of righteousness, God can't help but get the glory.

The song David was playing no doubt became a well-known psalm. Just imagine where your song, dance, shout, clap, preaching, teaching, and prophecy can end up and how many they will free.

Introduction

Mentoring through Prayer is a composite sketch, and portrait, of a time-honored institution known as intercessory prayer with a twenty-first-century twist and a twenty-first-century application.

The story of David playing the harp for Saul is our backdrop. The application and revelation to the churches and our church leaders is a stealth approach to mentoring, shaping, and molding our leaders through the intensity of prayer that produces evidenced based results. Of course none of this is of our own doing but through the Christ in us the hope of his Glory. In 1 Samuel 16:13, David is anointed the future king of Israel, and the spirit of the Lord comes upon him. In the very next verse (14), King Saul experiences the spirit of the Lord departing from him, thereby producing a distressing spirit. The next chain of events leads the current king to seek out an intercessor (the future king) to play the harp for him in the hopes that the distressing spirit or tormenting spirits will depart. Whether we know it or not, every leader called to shepherd God's sheep experiences the onslaught of distressing spirits/tormenting spirits that wreak havoc upon the soul and spirit of man. This ongoing spiritual warfare unfortunately comes with the territory of leadership/shepherding. Pastoring is one of the most stressful occupations in the world.

*Statistics on Pastors, (article) by Dr. Richard J. Krejcir:

After over eighteen years of researching pastoral trends, and many of us having firsthand pastoral experience, we have found that pastors are in a dangerous occupation! (This data is backed up by other studies.) We are perhaps the single most stressful and frustrating working profession, more than medical doctors, lawyers, politicians, or cat groomers (hey, they have to deal with claws). We found that over 70 percent of pastors are so stressed out and burned out that they regularly consider leaving the ministry. (I only feel that way on Mondays.) Thirty-five to 40 percent of pastors actually do leave the ministry, most after only five years. On a personal note, out of the twelve senior pastors that I have served under directly, two have passed away, and four have left the ministry totally—that is, not only are they no longer in the pulpit, but they no longer even attend a church.

*© 2007 (research from 1989 to 2006) R. J. Krejcir Ph.D. Francis A. Schaeffer Institute of Church Leadership Development

With this being said, these distressing spirits that affect our leaders produce on many occasions a church that looks to be scattered, fragmented, dysfunctional, debilitated, defective, flawed, maladjusted and wounded.

I believe every letter that apostle Paul wrote to the churches was his attempt to prevent a church with many dysfunctional symptoms. In other words, Paul wanted with all of his heart to eliminate a church with a major identity crisis.

So mentoring through prayer is a tool, an app, and even a possible curriculum to aid the sheep/laypeople/intercessors to pray with all power, soul, and might for their leaders to come into a place of peace, stability, and oneness with God.

Mentoring through prayer affords everyone the chance to be a (figurative) harp/lyre player. For many, harp/lyre playing looks like **intense** prayer- warfare (intercession), playing of instruments, singing in the spirit, shouting, clapping, jumping, worshiping, praising, writing, preaching, and teaching. David's playing the harp/lyre for Saul was the beginning of many psalms being written. His harp/lyre playing relieved many distressing spirits then, and his psalms relieve many distressing spirits for us all now.

Mentoring through prayer will reduce and hopefully eliminate the dysfunctions/ twelve transgressions mentioned in the book:

- Sheep Abuse
- Denominational Identity Crisis—Who Are We?
- Spiritual Infanticide
- Carnal Christianity
- Humpty-Dumpty Syndrome
- Financial Fatigue
- Pulpit Abuse
- Fear of the Supernatural Christ Anointing
- Fivefold-Office Annihilation
- Spiritual Gifts and Benediction
- Church-Membership Recidivism
- Salvation Deprivation

Two

TRADITIONAL MANTRAS

*M*any, many, many times throughout our Christian walk, we've used or heard the terms and phrases below. We are asked to pray with others, pray over others, pray others through a difficult time, pray against evil spirits and, last but not least, pray for those in need of a miracle and/or a breakthrough. Here are a few verses that are perfect in these circumstances:

Pray with: 1 Thessalonians 5:17

- Pray Over: James 5:14: "Let them call the elders of the church, and let them pray over them."
- Pray Through: Philippians 1:19
- Pray For: James 5:16: "Pray for one another that you may be healed."
- Pray against: Ephesians 6:10–11: "Finally, my brethren, be strong in the Lord and in the power of His might. Put on the whole armor of God that you may be able to stand against the wiles of the devil."
- Pray without ceasing: 1 Thessalonians 5:16–17: "Rejoice always, pray without ceasing."

- <u>Pray Continually</u>: Psalm 72:15: "And He shall live; and the gold of Sheba will be given to Him; prayer also will be made for Him continually, and daily He shall be praised."

Interestingly, I just purchased a William Murphy CD, and one of the songs is entitled "Praying for you." A great connection while writing. The concept/principle of prayer is a time-honored, time-tested practice. However, God asked me to write a book entitled Mentoring through Prayer. Or I should say, God wrote this book through me.

Much of what I've written, via the Holy Spirit, more than likely will be things you've heard or read before. However, I hope you receive the essence of what I've written as fresh, divine, Holy Spirit–inspired revelation.

My prayer is that this book will be a tool or an app, if you will, that you can and will download into your "heart drive" when things just appear discombobulated, funky, out of sorts, spirit grieving, and spirit quenching. Do not quench (suppress or subdue) the [Holy] Spirit 1 Thessalonians 5:19).

Three

The Need

I hear from saints all the time who say, "I believe I'm in the right house of worship, but I feel dead and unfulfilled; my spirit is grieved and dying. What do I do? I love my pastor, and I want to stay, but I'm not growing; I'm stagnant..." Yes, I hear these cries more than I would like. Unfortunately, this situation is common in the body of Christ and in the Kingdom of God.

Many Pastors and leaders called to the ministry—anointed and appointed by God—have a difficult time identifying the sheep among them and, more than that, identifying the Gifts and bestowals birthed in them, and given to them by God, before the foundations of the world.

This challenge, might I add, requires skill but is attainable. Identifying your sheep and their gifts requires hours and hours and hours of prayer and staying in God's face. Here's a theological (Theo-God, ology-Study of) buster: studying the scriptures will give you what you need to preach the Word on Sunday. Seeking God, communing with God, supping with God face-to-face, and wrestling with God as a daily regiment allows pastors and officers to supernaturally see into the spirit of their people (the sheep). Once you have that inside view, the Holy Spirit will identify their gifts and callings. Relationship, Relationship, Relationship.

After all, that's the objective of Ephesians chapter 4. Equipping is not just X's and O's on the blackboard. If that were the case, we wouldn't have so many athletes with calamitous lives that eventually lead to ruin.

Paul says in Romans 1:11, "I long to see you that I may impart spiritual gifts." Impart here is the key word.

"OK," I asked the Holy Spirit, "who will a book of this nature bless the most? Leadership, laity, or those called by God who are sitting and dying in the pews?"

One of the gravest injustices to the body of Christ I've experienced, over the past twenty-three years, is the failure to implement the "law of spiritual reproduction" found in 2 Timothy 2:2.

New King James Version (NKJV)

And the things that you have heard from me among many witnesses, commit these to faithful men who will be able to teach others also.

Amplified Bible (AMP)

And the [instructions] which you have heard from me along with many witnesses, transmit and entrust [as a deposit] to reliable and faithful men who will be competent and qualified to teach others also.

The Bible never teaches us to sit; it teaches us to go. But we sit and sit and sit and sit. Hundreds of churches throughout the body have not trained leaders to operate in their gifts (especially the office of the pastor). What happens if the pastor' dies or becomes incapacitated? Who will carry the torch, the mantle, the baton?

There are churches that found themselves in this dilemma and were relegated to listening to the former pastors' tapes/CD's/videos recordings. Are you kidding me?! Not one soul, in a full house, was able to carry the mantle?????

So what happens is, we become <u>cynical</u>, <u>critical</u>, <u>analytical</u>, <u>judgmental</u>, <u>hypocritical</u>, and <u>hypercritical</u>. How, why, and where did I come up with these terms, the Holy Spirit's rebuke of yours truly?

Because of the grace of God, I was blessed to be trained under one of God's fiercest generals. She was recently ordained as an apostle, and, yes, she wears the mantle and calling well. She trained not only myself, at least several hundred like myself over the years. She was and still is the epitome of 2 Timothy 2:2.

However, there was one major problem with being trained <u>under</u> and <u>by</u> such a great anointing, one becomes;

Cynical: doubting or contemptuous of human nature or the motives, goodness, or sincerity of others

Critical: 1. tending to find fault with somebody or something or with people and things in general; containing or involving comments and opinions that analyze or judge something, especially in a detailed way

Analytical: able or inclined to separate things into their constituent parts in order to study or examine them, draw conclusions, or solve problems

Judgmental: tending to judge or criticize the conduct of other people

Hypocritical: behaving in a way that suggests one has higher standards or more noble beliefs than is the case

Hypercritical: excessively and unreasonably critical, especially of small faults

After my wife and I parted ways from this particular ministry and leader, every other ministry and leader could not (in our eyes) meet the high standards, teaching, and anointing we had experienced. What a major dilemma. It's sort of like trying to live up to the standards of your significant other. Believe it or not, we never quite meet the bill, although our partners lead us to believe (many times) that we do.

What I'm saying I, that every ministry that my wife and I would visit, join, or help build would never quite meet the bill for us. Does this mean there are perfect ministries or churches? No way; perfection will only come when the Perfect One returns. 1 Corinthians 13: [9]for we know in part and we prophesy in part. [10]But when that which is perfect has come, then that which is in part will be done away.

So here's how it would normally play out. We would sit through the service (s) and analyze, analyze, analyze until we were blue in the face. Then I would become cynical, critical, judgmental, and hypercritical, the last being (criticizing somebody or something too severely or too much).

After several years of this pattern, God began to rebuke me severely. Who did I think I was—the authority on what a perfect ministry/church should look or be like? No, no, no. And then the Holy Spirit spoke to me and said, "You have mentored many men and women in ministry face-to-face with a hands-on approach. Now try mentoring through prayer behind the scenes."

The revelation and concept for the book came to me while reading 1 Samuel 16:13–23.

What has also been birthed out of this passage is what The Holy Spirit has identified as 12 Transgressions (to violate a law or command i.e. sin) that has caused extreme damage to our churches, the sheep and the body of Christ. Each of the 12 Transgressions takes a stethoscope look at the perils of inappropriate ministry committed upon the sheep in general and the church as a whole. If these 12 Transgressions are taken seriously and aggressively attacked, church autopsies will become a minimal thing of the past.

The First Transgression is "Sheep Abuse"; the number one, common transgression, in the Body of Christ. It speaks of the emotional, verbal, psychological, spiritual, financial and at times physical (sexual) atrocities perpetrated against and upon the congregants/sheep of God in the Church. We go to God via the Church to obtain help and healing with all of the above issues. But many times we find ourselves in worse shape than when we came.

The Second Transgression is "Denominational Identity Crisis"; it speaks of the Denominational dysfunctions and behaviors that have plagued the body of Christ for centuries. These disorders have produced thousands of different denominational and organizational titles. These dilemma's continue to produce the question, "Who are we"?

The Third Transgression is "Spiritual Infanticide"; A very harsh but descriptive term. Spiritual infants enter the church, receive salvation and find themselves left alone at the altar. What I've seen happen time after time is, young converts waiting to be discipled, thrown into an incubator-purgatory if you will. The people who are to disciple them are so busy with their own mundane everyday issues that they forget about the new babes. This leads to a spiritual infanticide or spiritual infant death syndrome. This chapter addresses the need to return to the real objective of the church and the "Great Commission", "Making Disciples of all Nations and people".

The Forth Transgression assesses (with a spiritual stethoscope) "Carnal Christianity". 1 Corinthian 3:3, for you are still carnal. For where there are envy, strife, and divisions among you, are you not carnal and behaving like mere men? What is "Carnal Christianity"? It's Christianity with a multiple personality syndrome. What does this mean? We publicly confess that we are Christians and behind the curtains we look just like the world (secular society). If we look like the world and act like the world what makes us different? This Chapter exposes the truth about Carnal Christianity and how we are to pray against its practice.

The Fifth Transgression focuses on the "Humpty Dumpty Syndrome"; we know the nursery rhyme, Humpty Dumpty sat on the wall, Humpty Dumpty had a great fall, all the Kings horses and all the Kings men couldn't put Humpty back together again". Our Pastors and Leaders climb the ladder of success and sit on the wall of success. We puff them up put them on a pedestal and make them little god's. The problem then becomes that we worship the creature rather than the Creator. This chapter exposes the dark nature of this transgression and how we are to pray for our Pastors and leaders to examine themselves with prayer solutions.

The Sixth Transgression probably focuses on the 2nd greatest pitfall of our Christian organizations/Churches, "Financial Fatigue"; in this chapter we take an in-depth look at the ways we give and why. Are we giving out of condemnation or are we giving because we are inspired by the Holy Spirit? Are we giving to please man or are we giving to please God. Are we giving to build God's Kingdom or are we giving to enhance man's kingdom? Are we sowing to Glorify God or sowing to glorify man? These questions and more will be answered in this insightful provocative chapter.

The Seventh Transgression "Pulpit Abuse" takes a close look at the inappropriate and improper practices being exercised or exorcised behind God's Holy Pulpit. Our job as we are taught in John 21:17, "to feed God's sheep". How and what we feed God's sheep should never ever be covered in a myriad of flesh. Personal use of God's pulpit was never ordained by Him. Misuse and Abuse leads too many fatalities. Mentoring Through Prayer is an attempt to "prevent the autopsy" of our churches before they die or the sheep die, under the practice, of the 12 Transgressions highlighted in each chapter. One example of misuse is when a Pastor or leader airs the dirty laundry of the sheep publicly. This also falls under the category of sheep abuse.

The Eighth Transgression "Fear of the Supernatural Christ Anointing" must be viewed with a very astute eye, open mind and heart. The Anointing of Christ must accompany God's ministers in order to produce the effective power and manifestation of God. This discussion will not only be thought provoking, it will be extremely controversial. Jesus himself received his power from on high in Matthew 3:15-16. It was the power from on High released from heaven that led Him into the wilderness and began His ministry with Power and anointing. Can we preach without the anointing? Yes! Will it be effective? You make the call. Do we fear the supernatural-anointing of Christ or are we content with the mediocre? You make the call! These questions and others will be addressed in this chapter.

The Ninth Transgression is the "Five Fold Ministry Annihilation". Catchy phrase, what does it mean? We understand God's intended purpose for growing the body of Christ and who He has chosen to do so. He clearly lays out His purpose and plan in the book of Ephesians Chapter 4 verses 11-12. Now just because we know His plan and understand it, it doesn't mean we fulfill its commitment.

In not fulfilling His commitment we undermine God by annihilating or cutting out several of the offices/officers and operate with one or two at the most. I believe with all my heart that God desires us to operate in His divine order. His divine order is that all Five Offices and Officers are operating within His Church and within the His Body, the body of Christ. Does your house of worship allow the operation of the Five Fold Ministry? If not, why or why not? Is it fear or lack of faith? Is it a lack of knowledge and or teaching on the Five Fold ministry? Are you asking questions or just going along with the program? You make the call! This chapter will provoke countless controversial responses.

The Tenth Transgression is near and dear to my heart; "Spiritual Gifts Benediction". Another catchy phrase that will be misunderstood my some but understood by many. Of course benediction connotes a sort of closing final prayer. It also may connote that something or someone has died. The essence of this transgression, speaks to the evident <u>movement</u> in parts of the body of Christ, to deny the supernatural power of God, that operates through the Gifts, given to us through His Son Jesus Christ. Yes these are strong allegations but very, very true.

In this chapter you will receive a concise breakdown of the gifts and a chart that will hopefully help you identify your gifts. You will learn how to pray against the benediction of the gifts and pray for the birthing of your own gifts, even when others can't see or identify them.

The Eleventh Transgression "Church Membership Recidivism" is a well-known and well discussed topic in the Body of Christ. Ok maybe the term recidivism is not common, however, church membership is a common discussion around the church coffee table. Church growth is a common topic but, how do we retain the members we have is a more pressing question. This chapter will try to answer the why's, how's, when's and where's of the seemingly <u>vacuum</u>, where members seem to exit.

Finally the Twelfth Transgression "Salvation Deprivation" is probably the most important Transgression of them all. Salvation and saving souls is the reason (or should be the main reason) why we become Christians. The word of God say's in Luke 19:10, "For the Son of Man came to seek and save the Lost." Seeking and saving the Lost is God's priority. Unfortunately it's not always our priority. Salvation has taken a back seat to; membership numbers, finances, entertainment, programs, and feel good messages. This chapter will take a microscopic look into why salvation has taken a back seat and how we can pray salvation back to the forefront of God's priority

My Best Friend, the Holy Spirit

The Holy Spirit, Comforter, Parakletos, Holy Ghost—whatever name you use to call him or describe him, he is real, and he is the third person of the Triune God. In the body of Christ, he is the missing link to our freedom and prosperity, spiritually, mentally, emotionally.

I can say with all honesty that I have a sincere and genuine relationship with the Holy Spirit. Most Christians have a relationship with Jesus but have never experienced a genuine relationship with the Holy Spirit and the Father. Because of the many books written about the Holy Spirit and the Father, I will not go in depth concerning the Person, Personality and Persona of the Holy Spirit and the Father. However, I will say that each person of the Trinity has a personality, a character, and a distinct persona, and each person of the Trinity perform different duties and tasks in our individual lives.

Scenario I

My first experience of mentoring through prayer began right after graduating from Teen Challenge (the most successful Christian rehabilitation center in the world). God spoke to me and commanded me to pray for, pray with, and pray over my best friend in Newark, New Jersey. We were friends together, athletes together, and drug addicts together. He always tells people that I led him to drugs and I led him to Christ. God told me to make sure I got my friend into and helped him get through Teen Challenge.

I don't know if Saul was smoking crack during his "distressing spirit" moments, but I do know that practicing a lifestyle of drugs, alcohol, and any other mind- and mood-altering substances is the epitome of **what a distressing spirit looks** and **acts like**. I came home, and my best friend was playing the Nation, the walls, and the hokey-pokey with the distressing spirits instructor (Satan). He would play hide-and-seek when I came to visit, peeping through the window blinds (with the crack pipe in his hands), and tell his brother to shoo me away. However, his attempts failed. I prayed and prayed and prayed and prayed until he received Christ, received the Holy Spirit, and eventually graduated from Teen Challenge. That was in 1992, and to this day he is going stronger than ever.

Application I

A relationship with the Holy Spirit will eliminate a mundane/perfunctory (: characterized <u>routine</u> or superficiality) Christian life. Many of us are content with church the usual versus church the unusual. We go to church every week, pay our tithes, participate in the building and maintenance of the church, sing in the choir, and attend classes, but we never ever really achieve the knock-down, drag-out, star spangled banner, breakthrough/fulfillment, waiting for every believer.

The Holy Spirit creates and produces an environment of unending excitement, fire, fireworks, miracles, signs, and wonders. Look at what happens in Matthew 3:13–17 and 4:1–11. After Jesus was baptized and filled with the Holy Spirit and led by the Spirit into the wilderness, the fireworks began. Nothing about these passages breeds dullness or boredom.

All of those mentioned earlier (those desiring or seeking more) are looking for the Matthew 3–4, book-of-Acts experience.

This book, however, is not just about the insecurities of the pastor/pastoral office; it is more about how we can mentor our pastors and leaders through prayer when we know there is more—more joy, more fulfillment, more excitement, more gifts, and more bestowals, more than just church as usual.

In 1991, while I was working for American Airlines (fresh out of Christian rehab and attending Bible college), one of my coworkers asked me if I would talk to (minister to) his sister. He said she was going to and attending a church and knew there had to be more than what she was experiencing. She felt religious but unfulfilled, dull, and mundane. She cried out, "There has to be more than this, and if something doesn't happen soon I will just stop going to church all together."

I began to minister to her by phone for nearly a year. One night, while I was praying for her to be filled with the Holy Ghost, bam! She began speaking in tongues. This infilling/indwelling went on for about thirty minutes; interestingly, at a later time, a few of her coworkers asked for the same indwelling, and it happened to them. Now the entire night shift (three or four ladies in total) was filled with the Holy Ghost, and their lives were never the same. She and her husband eventually came to the church I was attending. The greatest part of the story is that a year or two later she and her husband would bring my future wife to church with them. Yes, to this day we are seventeen years happily married and fulfilling God's call on our lives. The young lady and her husband have their own church and are fulfilling God's call on their lives as well.

What a difference the Holy Spirit makes in the lives of his people. Acts 1:8 says, "But you will receive power when the Holy Spirit comes on you, and you will be my witnesses in Jerusalem, and in all Judea and Samaria, and the ends of the earth."

Well, as you can tell by the story above, Acts 1:8 was manifested and fulfilled, and continues to be fulfilled through the writing of this book.

Scenario II

Yes, there are times when our leaders are approachable and display great listening skills. However, these occasions are few and far between. What am I talking about?

Pastors/leaders believe with all of their hearts that they hear from God and many times become offended when you begin to say "God/the Holy Spirit spoke to me concerning a matter." or even "May I share with you what God/the Holy Spirit is telling me?" Their defenses go up; the ego gets in the way, flesh abounds, and the congregant must resign to his or her corner until a clear path or window opens (if it opens at all). With this app, you will learn how to pry the window open.

The service begins; the cloud of smoke that has filled the temple is so thick that the pastor is caught up, the people are caught up, and the singers and musicians are caught up just as it is written in 2 Chronicles 5:12–14.

2 Chronicles 5:12–14 (NIV) All the Levites who were musicians—Asaph, Heman, Jeduthun, and their sons and relatives—stood on the east side of the altar, dressed in fine linen and playing cymbals, harps, and lyres. They were accompanied by 120 priests sounding trumpets. The trumpeters and musicians joined in unison to give praise and thanks to the Lord. Accompanied by trumpets, cymbals, and other instruments, the singers raised their voices in praise to the Lord and sang, "He is good; his love endures forever." Then the temple of the Lord was filled with the cloud, and the priests could not perform their service because of the cloud, for the glory of the Lord filled the temple of God.

But all of a sudden the pastor realizes that he or she is in service and decides the show (man designed program) must go on. "How dare the Holy Spirit takeover my service! After all, I've studied and researched for this message, and I have to deliver it. If I don't give my seven points and graphic alliterations, I may lose my anointing. I may lose my audience. I may lose my offering. I may lose my numbers. I may lose my mind."

(Alliteration is a poetic or literary effect achieved by using several words that begin with the same or similar consonants, as in "Whither wilt thou wander, wayfarer?")

OK, you're probably saying one of two things right about now: "I've experienced this a hundred times and was either grieved or baffled." or "Who does this preacher think he is talking about God's leaders like this?"

You see, I'm OK with who I am and whose I am, so I solicit and accept either response. Speaking from twenty-four years of experience kind of makes you an authority in these matters whether you want to be or not. All questions and comments are welcomed, contact information at the end of the book.

The idea of this book is to provoke and stimulate those who are dying in the maternity wards of the church to get angry enough to do something about such travesties. Yes, I said travesties. How long are we going to tell the Holy Spirit to sit down and shut up? That's essentially what we do when we say, "I'm the preacher; I've got to fulfill my calling and feed God's sheep, and no one, not even the Holy Spirit, will stop me." Ouch!

It may feel like I have deviated, but I haven't; I just had a few "glory filled the temple, and the preacher had to preach" flashbacks.

Has this happened? Yes.

Does this happen? Yes.

Will this continue to happen? Yes.

Can we help prevent this from happening? Yes, but only to a certain extent.

How? **By mentoring our pastors and leaders through prayer**. We must become instruments of righteous literally and figuratively. Romans 6:13 Do not **offer** any part **of** yourself to sin as an **instrument of** wickedness, but rather **offer** yourselves to God as those who have been brought from death to life; and **offer** every part **of** yourself to him as an **instrument of righteousness**.

As I said before, after twenty years of ministry—being used by God to build churches, ministries and mentor young pastors in the ministry—one sees the (from the inside and out) constant disenfranchisement of the person, personality, and persona of the Holy Spirit.

The high side of this is that I've seen what the results of mentoring through prayer can be. The low side is that we end up with contorted, paralyzed, unhealthy churches.

Let's define mentoring/mentor: A mentor is somebody, usually older and more experienced, who advises and guides a younger, less experienced person; a senior or experienced person in a company or organization who gives guidance and training to a junior colleague.

Now our mind-set tells us that this is an age-specific issue, but really it does not matter when, how old, or what grade the mentor is. The only thing that matters is that the mentor knows especially how to pray with the Word and how to pray with specifics.

For example: "Father, in the name of your son Jesus, I'm asking that you minister to our pastor with all power and clarity concerning the ministry, the person, personality, and persona of the Holy Spirit and that his power be manifested in our services. Father, we pray that he (the Holy Spirit) not be thwarted, diffused, grieved, quenched

(1 Thessalonians 5:19 Do not quench (suppress or subdue) the [Holy] Spirit), or blasphemed so that your power would bring forth healing, deliverance, salvation, freedom, and the birthing of your gifts upon and through your people. In Jesus's name, amen."

Matthew 12:31 says, "And so I tell you, every kind of sin and slander can be forgiven, but blasphemy against the Spirit will not be forgiven." Discussions and/or sermons concerning the Holy Spirit being blasphemed are pretty nonexistent. As a matter of fact, I can't remember the last message/discussion initiated on this topic in the last several years.

The Holy Ghost and the fivefold ministry are the forgotten children of the body of Christ. They all involve the supernatural manifestation of God. Unfortunately, Hollywood has taken over the supernatural. So it is our job to do our part to help the fivefold ministry (especially the prophet and apostle) to regain their footing/rightful place in the kingdom of God.

This discussion, however, I will save for the next book. The point of the above paragraph is to note that the Holy Spirit, the supernatural, the fivefold offices, and mentoring through prayer are synonymous to a great extent.

I recently engaged in a conversation with an associate pastor who has a big role in the beginning of each service at a mega-church. He began to convey how he loves his pastor and church but has of late been grieved, frustrated, and saddened by the blanketing of the Comforter (how's that for an oxymoron). He went on to say that in several services, where the Holy Spirit was so involved in bringing fire to the service, he unfortunately has had to stop the flow of the service make eye contact with the pastor to solicit his approval or disapproval.

The pastor in turn would make facial gestures while gazing at his watch. Of course, out of obedience, honor, and respect, the associate pastor had to obey and bring the worship/glory experience to a screeching end. How painful is that? Very, very, very painful.

Can you envision the Holy Spirit and how he must have been feeling? It's sort of the countenance one sees when a child is told to go to his room.

By now, those of you reading this who have the baptism of the Holy Ghost should be saying that mentoring through prayer should be activated and implemented if and when the Holy Spirit is not activated and present in that particular leader or church.

Am I saying pastors, ministers, fivefold leaders, and the like don't have the Holy Spirit? No; on the contrary, the question is not whether they have the Holy Spirit but rather, **<u>why the Holy Spirit is being ignored</u>**.

Believe it or not, there are men and women of God (who have the Holy Spirit with the evidence of speaking in tongues) who frequent casinos and play the lottery; however, they ignore the unction of the Holy Spirit.

1 John 2:20

But ye have unction from the Holy One, and ye know all things.

We're all guilty of this at one time or another because we all fall short of the glory of God. However, when the Father wants to accomplish something major via the Holy Spirit, it's up to us to have a spirit of discernment, follow his leading, and allow him to be manifested in our lives for the glory of the Father.

John 16:13

Howbeit, when he, the Spirit of truth, has come, he will guide you into all truth; for he will not speak on his own authority, but whatever he hears he will speak; and he will tell you things to come.

Prayer Defined

This Chapter is devoted to a partially in-depth study of the word prayer. Everyone is not nor will be a biblical scholar so this chapter does some of the leg work for them. However, on your own time please research for yourself.

Pray with: The Bible tells us to pray without ceasing

1 Corinthians 14:15 says, "So what shall I do? I will pray with my spirit, but I will also pray with my understanding."

Philippians 1:4-6 says, "In all my prayers for all of you, I always pray with joy because of your partnership in the gospel from the first day until now, being confident of this, that he who began a good work in you will carry it on to completion until the day of Christ Jesus."

Prayer: a spoken or unspoken address to God, a deity, or a saint. It may express praise, thanksgiving, confession, or a request for something such as help or somebody's well-being. Prayer is mentioned over 121 times in the NIV and 184 times in the NKJV.

Prayer: (a) Dar-ash (Hebrew)

to resort to, seek, seek with care, enquire, require), frequent (a place), (tread a place) to consult, enquire of, seek heathen gods, necromancers to seek deity in prayer and worship 1a God 1a heathen deities to seek (with a demand), demand, require to investigate, enquire to ask for, require, demand to practice, study, follow, seek with application to seek with care, care for (Niphal) to allow oneself to be enquired of, consulted (only of God) to be sought, be sought out to be required (of blood)

Prayer: (b) Hamah (Hebrew)

to murmur, growl, roar, cry aloud, mourn, rage, sound, make noise, be clamorous, be disquieted, be loud, be moved, be troubled, be in an uproar, (of a mob in prayer) be in a stir, be in a commotion be boisterous, be turbulent

Biblical imagery: Mentoring through prayer shows how Praying with or for someone looks through biblical imagery.

1 Samuel 16:14 Now the Spirit of the Lord had departed from "Saul, and an evil spirit from the Lord tormented him."

Two supernatural occurrences took place. Use your imagination for a minute the way Hollywood portrays evil spirits or good spirits leaving the body of a person. Visually you may see a silhouette of a spirit (some may even call a ghost) but it's a supernatural occurrence. In the New Testament Mark 5:25-34 a woman with and infirmity touched the hem of his garment and He said the "power had gone out of Him. The women received a healing because of this exchange.

Recognizing Where We Fall Short In This Fiasco

Recognizing where we fall short in this fiasco is very crucial to our understanding the need for mentoring through prayer. It may sound like I'm deviating from the topic, however, I'm not. Why does the Spirit of the Lord leave Saul? Why did he need someone to play the Harp/lyre for him? Why do we feel like the spirit of the Lord leaves us at times? Why do we feel tormented at other times? The why's are not always as important as the when's. We may never know why, but we do know when it happens, we need a Harp player, an intercessor to intercede on our behalf. We need someone to be and "Instrument" of righteousness (Romans 6:13).

Our cries for help and acknowledgment (where we fall short) must also require a magnifying glass/MRI approach. A self-examination if you will. What I'm trying to say is, that it's not always the church or the church leadership, it's us.

Seeing where we fall short, underachieve, breech our spiritual birth, shackled by fear, listen to soothsayers, walk in the counsel of the ungodly, stand in the path of sinners, and sit in the seat of the scornful is necessary. Yes, many of us have not made it to the promised land of our calling because of fear and trepidation.

Where did Saul fall short? Rebellion and Disobedience!
1 Samuel 15:23

For rebellion is as the sin of witchcraft, and stubbornness is as iniquity and idolatry. Because you have rejected the word of the Lord, He also has rejected you from being king."

Saul was asked by God to perform a certain task with due diligence. Saul chose to complete the task his way and not Gods way.

Many of us have gone to great churches, sat under great teaching and preaching, baptized and filled with the Holy Ghost, and heard God call us, but we've allowed spiritual apathy, lethargy, procrastination, rebellion and fear to <u>cement</u> us to our seat of destiny.

We transition from one church to another (in a different state, town, or city), sit/hide in the back of the church, and hope that the pastor/leaders pull us up and out of the pews. Many times we allow them to do so. We then become great church workers but never fulfill our real purpose, destiny, and calling. Miscarriage, missed opportunities, miseducation and rebellion—take your pick.

Mentoring through prayer transforms not only the pastors but also the church. When the church is transformed, the members ultimately are transformed. Picture a completely transformed (not perfect) church. Gifts are operating and flowing; officers and offices are in place and in operation. What is this called? The church in divine order.

Ministries, Gifts, and Activities

1 Corinthians 12:4-6

1) Now there are various kinds of gifts but the same Spirit.
2) There are various kinds of service and the same Lord.
3) There are various kinds of workings but the same God who works all things in all

Why insert this passage? These are the areas (never fully developed) that are usually the diseased symptoms of a unhealthy church.

All gifts are given to us from Jesus to operate in the body. These gifts are not exclusively for the pastor. But we presume them on the pastor. Why? Why? Why?

Because they are presumed on the pastor they are never fully developed or developed at all.

And then there are the fivefold offices; he gave some to be apostles; some, prophets; some, evangelists; and some, shepherds/pastors and teachers. These offices are also not exclusively for the pastor but for those who are called from birth in their mother's womb.

Jeremiah 1:5: "Before I formed you in the womb I knew you, before you were born I set you apart appointed you as a prophet to the nations."

The lack of teaching and training has placed these gifts, offices, and operations in a religious abyss. Servants like me are called to rehab, uncover, and reveal (not just in a pre-class cursory introduction) the gifts of God and the offices of God (especially the apostle and prophet).

Romans 12:4–8: "For as we have many members in one body, but all the members do not have the same function, so we, being many, are one body in Christ, and individually members of one another. Having then gifts differing according to the grace that is given to us, let us use them: if prophecy, let us prophesy in proportion to our faith; or ministry, let us use it in our ministering; he who teaches, in teaching; he who exhorts, in exhortation; he who gives, with liberality; he who leads, with diligence; he who shows mercy, with cheerfulness."

Mentoring through prayer is a results- and success-based book/principle. When looked upon with great scrutiny and applied results will be achieved.

For answers on why Saul asked specifically for a Harp/Lyre player read 1 Samuel Chapter 10.

Twelve Transgressions That Are Prevented through Mentoring through Prayer

- Sheep Abuse
- Denominational Identity Crisis—Who Are We?
- Spiritual Infanticide
- Carnal Christianity
- Humpty-Dumpty Syndrome
- Financial Fatigue
- Pulpit Abuse
- Fear of the Supernatural Christ Anointing
- Fivefold-Office Annihilation
- Spiritual Gifts Benediction
- Church-Membership Recidivism
- Salvation Deprivation
- Grace and Mercy—Not a License to Sin
- Prayer and Intercession Are War

Six

SHEEP ABUSE

Jeremiah 23:1–2: "'Woe to the shepherds who are destroying and scattering the sheep of my pasture!' Declares the Lord. Therefore this is what the Lord, the God of Israel, says to the shepherds who tend my people: 'because you have scattered my flock and driven them away and have not bestowed care on them, I will bestow punishment on you for the evil you have done,' declares the Lord."

Jeremiah 23:11: "'Both prophet and priest are godless; even in my temple I find their wickedness,' declares the Lord."

If you were to take a survey of how many sheep/saints have experienced sheep abuse, it would reach into the thousands and perhaps even millions.

Much of sheep abuse has occurred because of miseducation and/or lack of education. Many self-appointed pastors, prophets, and apostles may have heard the calling but not gone through nor received the rigorous training required.

Why is that important? You find out that the key ingredient is to have a shepherd's/pastor's heart.

However, I'm learning that even as I'm writing this book that there is a difference between pastoring and shepherding. Most pastors are equipped with a high level of the gift of administration. They have a corporate mindset and ability to run a business and manage people. This makes running and managing a church fairly easy. The downside is that they lack in the compassion department, the tenderhearted department, the unconditional love department. They are very good with the rod and the staff for pushing, prodding, and chastening, but they lack in using the rod and staff to gather for mending, healing, and applying the balm of Gilead for the healing of one's soul.

1 Samuel 16:7: "But the Lord said to Samuel, 'Do not look at his appearance or at his physical stature, because I have refused him. For the Lord does not see as man sees; for man looks at the outward appearance, but the Lord looks at the heart.'"

It's the heart of the shepherd that produces compassion, although the shepherd must also tend the sheep with his rod and his staff. The history of sheep abuse in the church/kingdom of God on earth has been ongoing since the inception of the church.

The irony of this discussion is the mere reality that most sheep are more severely hurt while in church than they are prior to their arrival.

I hate to establish the fact that I'm an authority on sheep abuse. However, my wisdom and authority comes from personal experience and identification. Yes, I've been a victim, up close and personal. It hurts; it rocks your world, your belief and faith system. Yes, a lot of this chapter is born out of my wife's and my own personal story.

Here's how it went. One Sunday the members of our church arrived at church to only receive a letter saying that the church was now officially closed. Most, if not all, of us were devastated. We poured our lives, hearts, blood, sweat, tears, and finances into this ministry for about five years, and now the doors were closed. Granted, it was the best Christian education I received; it's what has most enabled me to write this book. Our pastor was and is phenomenal, a great leader for God, but the closing of the church doors without prior notification was debilitating, demoralizing, and emotionally draining. And as I previously iterated, it took many of us up to five years to overcome.

Because I was the closest to the pastor, I was prophetically privy to the closing of the church prior to its closing. What does that mean? God revealed to me that the pastor set the wheels in motion for a new ministry (on paper) even before our church's closing. So this prophetic insight softened the blow and allowed me (as much as I could) to warn many who I had invited to the church. However, the healing of my wife was arduous and long. After all, she came to the church broken and need of healing. And now the shepherd assigned to the task of helping her, through healing process, had victimized the victim. Wow that could be a chapter within itself: "Hurting the Healed."

In that circumstance, I learned not only the meaning of "sheep abuse" but also the dos and don'ts of ministry.

A lot of the damage is a result of our own inability to discern our worship of the "creation versus the Creator".

The scripture says in Psalm 118:8–9 that it is better to trust in the Lord than to put confidence in man. It is better to trust in the Lord than to put confidence in princes.

Yes, God gave us pastors for the edification of the body but not for us to worship them. Sheep abuse is still abuse nonetheless. However, the blows could be lessened when our perspectives are prioritized: God, family, and ministry.

MARKS OF THE TRUE SHEPHERD

- Concern for the sheep
- Dutiful vigilance
- Perseverance
- Return of the rescued
- Godly nourishment
- Conscientious preservation
- Providing of proper spiritual rest
- Healing
- Mending
- Singleness of service
- Attentiveness
- Promotion and release of blessing
- Enabling of abundant life
- Enabling of liberation
- Furnishing of security
- Enrichment of redemption
- Diligence in service
- Sheep gathering
- Rescue of lost and bound
- Holy nurturing
- Adequate pasturing
- Faithful care
- Search for strays
- Reparation
- Defense of the threatened and vulnerable
- Devotion to flock and God
- Sacrifice
- Provisions of covenant
- Establishment of safety
- Enabling joy of freedom
- Release of enslaved possessions
- Fostering of godly satisfaction

Opposites of a True Shepherd

- Feeding of self and not flock
- Self-indulgence
- Gluttony and insatiability
- Dereliction
- Indifference to flock needs
- Cruelty
- Reckless endangerment of flock
- Extraordinary extravagance
- Neglectfulness
- Abandonment of flock
- Obliviousness to flock suffering
- Selfishness
- Insensitivity to God and church[1]

---

1 Paula A Price, "Marks of a True Shepherd. "Price, Dr. Paul A. 1994. The Five-Fold Ministry Offices, *Ephesians 4:11-12*. Flaming Vision Publication (pg. 150)

Sheep abuse like domestic violence comes in many forms: Mental, physi-cal, emotional, verbal, sexual, financial, spiritual, and psychological, with many times long lasting effects. One highly publicized act of abuse was a Pastor with HIV-AIDS who knowingly slept with several members of his congregation. The lasting effects of this abuse can have long lasting irreparable harm. The list of abuses are numerous and would more than likely open the wounds of some who are reading this book. My purpose was not to open wounds but to close them and provide prayer and insight to eradicate this behavior.

The healing process for sheep who have suffered abuse, misuse, hurt, and outright devastation usually takes between one too five years. A loving church with a healing touch and a loving support system will also be need-ed and highly recommended.

Example prayer for prevention of sheep abuse:

Father, in the name of Jesus, you know the devastating effects of sheep abuse perpetrated against your sheep. We need and call on your divine, su-pernatural intervention to first reveal when, where, and how these abomi-nations occur. Then we ask that you perform supernatural heart surgery on our pastors/leaders who willfully commit these abominable atrocities. Father, make your altar their resting place where transgressions and in-iquities die, where flesh dies, where carnality dies, where egos die, where insensitivities become sensitive, and uncompassionate becomes compas-sionate. Father, heal them and transform them in your heart and image. In Jesus name, amen.

Seven

DENOMINATIONAL IDENTITY

CRISES—WHO ARE WE?

Acts 19:13–16

> Some Jews who went around driving out evil spirits tried to invoke the name of the Lord Jesus over those who were demon-possessed. They would say, "In the name of the Jesus whom Paul preaches, I command you to come out." Seven sons of Sceva, a Jewish chief priest, were doing this. One day the evil spirit answered them, "Jesus I know, and Paul I know about, but who are you?" Then the man who had the evil spirit jumped on them and overpowered them all. He gave them such a beating that they ran out of the house naked and bleeding.

Many churches suffer from an identity crisis. In Wikipedia, the statistical numbers say that there are 33,000 denominations in the world. Baptist, Church of God in Christ, Church of Christ, Church of God, Catholic, nondenominational, Seventh-Day Adventist, Jehovah's Witness, Lutheran, Vineyard, Assemblies of God, Episcopalian, Presbyterian, Methodist, African Methodist Episcopal, and the list goes on and on.

Who are we? Denominational roots usually cloud the identity process. A desire to go where God wants us to go—thinking out of the box, if you will—becomes forestalled by our allegiance to our roots. In one service alone we accommodate at least three religions/denominations. In the morning, we cater to a more traditional service, and in the afternoon we cater to the contemporary generation. The third service is somewhere in between.

One Sunday, we believe in the supernatural signs, wonders, and miracles of God, and the next Sunday we tell the Holy Spirit to sit in time-out so the preacher can get his points across.

When are we?

One week we focus on salvation, and the next week we focus on church membership. In another service we have four to five separate altar invitations.

What takes place is the salvation invitation gets completely muddied, muddled, and confused. God has a plan of salvation, and we opt for a plan of membership.

Allegiance to the way we used to do things keeps us bound in and to the proverbial religious-traditional box (a practice I call **boxology**). This is what apostle Paul fought against over and over again.

Mark 7:13: "Making the word of God of no effect through your tradition, which you have handed down. And many such things you do."

Fresh ideas, fresh approaches, and fresh revelations are what God's people are seeking and are desperately in need of. Not more <u>boxology</u> religion and tradition. Mentoring through prayer will dispel, tear down, uproot, and destroy the shackles and yokes of religion. We have to become box cutters, cutting and destroying all the boxes that have stifled and stagnated us into a religious purgatory, if you will.

<u>Boxology</u> is the inability to think outside of the box, the norm, what seems right, the way we've always done it, and my-way ministries, Religionnnnnnnnn, law, legalism, "program hell," "order of service abyss."

<u>Religious abyss</u> is a place where witchcraft and sorcery are incubated (as in the development of an infectious disease). What does this

mean? The Abyss is defined as Hell or the bottom of the sea/ocean. Religion and Tradition are stifling our churches. The Church God intended wasn't for the development of religion and tradition, it was so Gods sheep would develop a relationship with Him. It's never been about organized religion it's always been about relationship, relationship, relationship. Religious Abyss is where religious clicks are formed that eventually have the appearance of a sort of witchcraft and or sorcery. They produce division, dissension, fear, gossip, discord, rebellion, conflict, and eventually opposition to Gods purposes and plans. Psalms 1 verse 2 says it better than I can:

Psalm 1:2[a]

> [1] Blessed (happy, fortunate, prosperous, and enviable) is the man who <u>walks</u> and lives <u>not</u> in the counsel of the ungodly [following their advice, their plans and purposes], <u>nor</u> stands [submissive and inactive] in the path where sinners walk, <u>nor</u> sits down [to relax and rest] where the scornful [and the mockers] gather.
>
> Where ever these are (ungodly, sinners, scornful) witchcraft is brewing.

A spirit of delusion is also incubated:

> Delusion: something that is falsely or deceitfully believed or propagated; b) a persistent false, psychotic belief regarding the self, persons, or objects outside the self that is maintained despite indisputable evidence to the contrary;

c) The abnormal state marked by such beliefs

False religions (i.e., divination and all the abominable practices listed in Deuteronomy 18) are formed in a religious-traditional incubator that <u>binds the human soul</u>, causing a <u>spiritual paralysis</u>. Jesus encountered spiritual and physical paralysis on a daily basis, caused part and parcel by the Sadducees and Pharisees religious and traditional practices. This statement is sure to ruffle theological feathers!

Deuteronomy 18:9–14: "When you come into the land, which the Lord your God is giving you, you shall not learn to follow the abominations of those nations. There shall not be found among you anyone who makes his son or his daughter pass through the fire, or one who practices <u>witchcraft</u>, or a <u>soothsayer</u>, or one who <u>interprets omens,</u> or a <u>sorcerer,</u> or one who <u>conjures spells,</u> or a <u>medium,</u> or a <u>spiritist,</u> or one who calls up the dead (<u>necromancer</u>). For all who do these things are an abomination to the Lord, and because of these abominations the Lord your God drives them out from before you. You shall be blameless before the Lord your God. For the nations, which you will dispossess, listened to soothsayers and diviners; but as for you, the Lord your God has not appointed such for you."

Proverbs 14:12 (AMP): "There is a way that seems right to a man and appears straight before him, but at the end of it is the way of death."

Religion and tradition become so perfunctory (characterized by routine or superficiality) that what looks like God, worship, praise, or God's glory is a manufactured, bastardized facsimile of Christianity called paganism.

On the flip side of all this are the denominations or nondenominational churches whose freedom to worship, praise, sing, dance, clap, and play instruments—everything that God says is his delight—mirrors true worship.

I remember that when I first received the gift of salvation, I was told about churches in Newark, New Jersey, that would not allow instruments in the church. The instruments were identified as tools of the devil. I couldn't wrap my head around this enigma. I read over and over again that we're to make a joyful noise unto the Lord. And then there is the Apostolic faith, which didn't allow the wearing of makeup, jewelry, and, for females, pants; any form of what's considered worldly activity or attire was completely disallowed. Don't get me wrong; this book is not solely about legalism, religion, and tradition. But it's about shining a light on the <u>BOXES</u>, restraints, bonds, fetters, shackles, chains, and yokes we find ourselves entrapped in.

With the effective application of mentoring through prayer, all of the above can be broken, destroyed, and removed. A place and atmosphere of freedom will be the ultimate achievement.

THIS MAY BE REPEATED SEVERAL TIMES IN THE PAGES AHEAD-THE PURPOSE OF MENTORING THROUGH PRAYER IS TO RAISE UP AN ARMY OF INTERCESSORS WHO WILL MENTOR OUR PASTORS, LEADERS AND MINISTERS INTO A VICTORY OVER THE 12 TRANSGRESSIONS.

John 4:23–24: "But the hour is coming, and now is, when the true worshipers will worship the Father in spirit and truth; for the Father is seeking such to worship him. God is spirit, and those who worship him must worship in spirit and truth." Spirit and truth are synonymous to freedom.

2 Corinthians 3:6: "Who also made us sufficient as ministers of the new covenant, not of the letter but of the Spirit; for the letter kills, but the Spirit gives life." This verse says it all: Spirit and truth are synonymous to life. The letter of the law and the law of the letter are synonymous to that which binds and kills. Jesus says, "I come so that you may have life and life more abundantly." He doesn't say, "I come that you may be bound and bound more abundantly to the law, like a boa constrictor."

Example prayer for escaping RELIGIOUS-BOXOLOGY:

Father we pray for your pastors, ministers, and leaders, of your church to be armed with **spiritual box-cutting tools**, destroying any and all traditional and religious mind-sets holding your people captive. Father, when religion exalts itself against the knowledge of God, teach us how to cut through that box. When the traditions of men exalt themselves against the knowledge of God, teach us how to cut through these boxes. Father, your Word says in 2 Corinthians 3:17 that you are the Spirit, and wherever your spirit is there is liberty (emancipation from bondage and freedom). Emancipate us, God; emancipate our leaders, pastors, and ministers who have not seen the light of liberty, the light of freedom, the light of your strong tower, where we can run to and be safe. Teach us, Father, that whom your son set free is free indeed, and teach us how to walk in that freedom. In Jesus's name, amen.

Eight

SPIRITUAL INFANTICIDE

Jeremiah 23:1-2

"Because you have scattered my flock and driven them away and have not bestowed care on them, I will bestow punishment on you for the evil you have done," declares the Lord.

"Aftercare" is a term we throw around haphazardly. We bring souls into the kingdom, give them a few classes, and drop them without fully nurturing them.

This may sound extremely harsh, but I'm defining infanticide in this context as the "killing of infants"—not physically, but spiritually. Leaving a newborn/born-again babe in Christ to fend for him- or herself is a form of spiritual infanticide. Deuteronomy 18:10a says, "Let no one be found among you who sacrifices his or her son or daughter in the fire." This scripture literally speaks of the practice of Old Testament infanticide. However, it doesn't specifically give an age. But it does talk about literally sacrificing children to the gods of Baal. The point is that we are to feed the sheep, not sacrifice them. Sometimes young sheep have a bottle of milk jammed in their mouths; sometimes the milk is too cold and/or produces colic. Babes left unattended during a crying spell can also be damaged. Many times a bottle is given without a label to identify feeding instructions. OK, many young parents have been taught few or zero parenting skills. It's no different with pastoring. Parenting and pastoring are synonymous.

Pastors who are called sometimes have the skill set but not the heart of compassion, or vice versa. What does this mean?

Pastors, like parents, need teaching and training (and not just on-the-job training). Classroom training with experienced seasoned pastors is highly recommended. Bishop T. D. Jakes always comes to mind when having these kinds of discussions. Bishop Jakes has realized the need and always designs leadership-mentoring conferences to teach pastors how to pastor and leaders how to lead. Sometimes we have to put our egos aside and recognize that we need help. This is where mentoring through prayer comes in.

Young converts, young sheep, spiritual infants, and new babes in Christ do not have to die. They can live a life of maturity and victory. It is our job, especially the shepherd, to nurture and feed the sheep. Some people assume that sheep are dumb and need to have their hands held through their entire walk. Not always the case. Most spiritual infants, like those in the NA and AA movements, need a solid foundation, a support system—what the NA/AA movement calls a sponsor. They need someone whom they can call when feeling attacked, weak, harassed, tormented, out of sorts, vulnerable, and tempted beyond their ability to be unyielding.

Where are we? What are we doing or not doing?

Now that you're a spiritual giant, a mature saint, a seasoned saint, and a Bible-totting, tongue-talking, demon-chasing beast, your job doesn't end there.

And just because your congregation is large in number doesn't mean you can't take a call and rescue the wounded, broken, battered, raped, addicted, and newly born.

Hospital visits are easy and self-aggrandizing, but taking time to pick up the lost with broken limbs and placing them on your back is difficult.

Their bills may be paid, and the outside may look fabulous. But the truth of the matter is that the inside is jacked up, busted, suicidal, broken, or on the brink of some sort of breakdown (such as a marriage in shambles). And the pastors and leadership are totally oblivious to it all.

The worst thing any newborn can hear on the other end of the phone line (from an old or new saint) is "Oh, you have to make an appointment to see the pastor; his schedule is full, so we will get back to you."

Or how about this: the pastor is experiencing the same trauma you're experiencing and avoids meeting with you because of his own insecurities.

OK, that's too deep; I will save that for the next book. The point is that it's not about the point; it's about the person. The Bible clearly says to feed the sheep in both the Old and New Testament (Ezekiel and the book of John). Sometimes the sheep just want the loving, caring hand of the shepherd-pastor. Check out this appropriate barn burner:

The Message Bible version below,

Ezekiel 34:1, 7, 10: "God's message came to me: 'Son of Man, prophesy against the shepherd-leaders of Israel. Yes, prophesy! Tell those shepherds God, the Master, says, "Doom to you shepherds of Israel, feeding your own mouths! Aren't shepherds supposed to feed sheep? You drink the milk, you make clothes from the wool, you roast the lambs, but you don't feed the sheep. You don't build up the weak ones, don't heal the sick, don't doctor the injured, don't go after the strays, and don't look for the lost. You bully and badger them. And now they're scattered every which way because there was no shepherd—scattered and easy pickings for wolves and coyotes. Scattered—my sheep!—exposed and vulnerable across mountains and hills. My sheep scattered all over the world, and no one out looking for them!"'

"Therefore, shepherds, listen to the Message of God: 'As sure as I am the living God—Decree of God, the Master—because my sheep have been turned into mere prey, into easy meals for wolves, because you shepherds ignored them and only fed yourselves, listen to what God has to say: "Watch out! I'm coming down on the shepherds and taking my sheep back. They're fired as shepherds of my sheep. No more shepherds who just feed themselves! I'll rescue my sheep from their greed. They're not going to feed off my sheep any longer!'"'"

Ezekiel 34:20: "Therefore, God, the Master, says, 'I myself am stepping in and making things right between the plump sheep and the skinny sheep. Because you forced your way with shoulder and rump and butted at all the weaker animals with your horns till you scattered them all over the hills, I'll come in and save my dear flock, no longer let them be pushed around. I'll step in and set things right between one sheep and another.'"

Well, as you can see in these verses, God takes this matter very seriously. Mentoring through prayer will allow you and your pastor to receive wise counseling from God on how to properly and adequately shepherd the sheep of God. This may sound harsh, but some churches are mausoleums where sheep (especially young lambs) go to die.

Example prayer for shepherding:

Father, we pray that the shepherding compassion of the Father's heart captures and recaptures the compassion of the pastor and leaders of your church on earth. Let the mercy of Jesus Christ and favor of the Holy Spirit saturate the heart of your pastors and leaders assigned to feed your sheep. Let these prayers be like a tsunami of love wrapped around their heart of hearts. Let your unconditional love be their resting place, their pillow during sleepless nights, and the tapestry sown throughout their spiritual being. Father, as you sent your Son to provide salvation, allow your salvation and the feeding of your sheep to be their utmost priority. Father, conform our pastors and leaders to your will and not their own. When selfish, diabolical self-aggrandizement obstructs the view of our pastors and leaders and their ability to feed your sheep, rebuke and chasten them with stern authority, as only you can. In the name of Jesus Christ, amen.

Hebrews 12:10–11: "For our earthly fathers disciplined us for only a short period of time and chastised us as seemed proper and good to them; but He disciplines us for our certain good, that we may become sharers in

His own holiness. For the time being, no discipline brings joy but seems grievous and painful; but afterward it yields a peaceable fruit of righteousness to those who have been trained by it a harvest of fruit, which consists in righteousness—in conformity to God's will in purpose, thought, and action, resulting in right living and right standing with God."

Nine

CARNAL CHRISTIANITY

Carnal: earthly, fleshly, material, mundane, sublunary (belonging to this world as opposed to the kingdom of God), temporal, terrestrial, worldly.

The word "carnality" comes from the Greek word "sarkikos," which in English connotes rotten flesh; Anti-spiritual in nature, this spirit appeals to the appetite of the soul.

Isaiah 29:8 (NIV)
> As when a hungry person dreams of eating, but awakens hungry still; as when a thirsty person dreams of drinking, but awakens faint and thirsty still. So will it be with the hordes of all the nations that fight against Mount Zion.

Beyoncé, Jay Z, Kanye West, and many of the idols of the entertainment industry have infiltrated Christendom at an alarming speed.

Lusts are evil desires that readily express themselves in bodily activities. They are the (so-called) natural tendency of the flesh and the soulish capacity and proclivity to gravitate toward things that are evil. Some lusts may characteristically be refined as in the pride of life, but they are still lusts.

Desire in and of itself is not to be feared. God promises us the desires of our hearts in the Psalm 37:4. Lust, prevails in our lives, we may get what we want, but we will lose what we have.[2]

Romans 8:6–8: "For to be carnally minded is death, but to be spiritually minded is life and peace. Because the carnal mind is enmity against God; for it is not subject to the law of God, nor indeed can be. So then, those who are in the flesh cannot please God."

Colossians 3:1–6: "If then you were raised with Christ, seek those things that are above, where Christ is, sitting at the right hand of God. Set your mind on things above, not on things on the earth. For you died, and your life is hidden with Christ in God. When Christ, who is our life, appears, then you also will appear with him in glory. Therefore put to death your members that are on the earth: fornication, uncleanness, passion, evil desire, and covetousness, which is idolatry. Because of these things the wrath of God is coming upon the sons of disobedience."

We have allowed Hollywood, social media, and the sports-entertainment industry to dictate what we would like to frame as a balanced lifestyle. We use the statement "We are in the world but not of the world" (1 Peter 2:11 [Living Before the World] Beloved, I beg you as **sojourners** and pilgrims (meaning we're not here to stay just passing through), abstain from fleshly lusts which war against the soul,) (as a catchy phrase, as opposed to taking it seriously and applying it to our lives. "We have to get to a place where we not only know the Word of God but also know the God of the Word".

When our favorite TV show is more controversial than the Word of God and the "God of the Word", carnal Christianity becomes more

---

2 Rules Of Engagement: The Art of Strategic Prayer and Spiritual Warfare
Dr. N. Cindy Trimm Creation House (pg. 171)

dominant than true Christianity. When our favorite team's schedule sets the priority for our church attendance, carnal Christianity becomes the dominant force. When only secular music is played at our church picnics, carnal Christianity has become the dominant force.

Author and Pastor Dr. Cindy Trimm has a book entitled When Kingdoms Clash. The title alone speaks volumes about what Christians and the body of Christ encounter on a daily basis.

The kingdom of light is clashing with the kingdom of darkness and it appears to be that no one is noticing. Looking like the World and acting like the World has become and acceptable norm or as the buzz phrase says, "The new normal".

Paul teaches us in Romans 6:11–14 that "in the same way, count yourselves dead to sin but alive to God in Christ Jesus. Therefore, do not let sin reign in your mortal body so that you obey its evil desires. Do not offer any part of yourself to sin as an instrument of wickedness, but rather offer yourselves to God as those who have been brought from death to life; and offer every part of yourself to him as an instrument of righteousness. For sin shall no longer be your master, because you are not under the law, but under grace."

We are supposed to be dead to sin, but we keep flirting with the things of the world, opening doors/portals to sin i.e. pornography, witchcraft, sorcery, the list goes on and on. Paul continues his dialogue with the battle of our sinful nature in Romans chapters 6, 7, and 8. This battle and these chapters, along with the topics of holiness and sanctification, have become forbidden in the "new age, seeker-friendly" church/environment.

What am I saying, and why?

Mentoring through prayer can reveal the transgressions of carnal Christianity. Once it is exposed, it will be eradicated. According to James 1:15, if carnal Christianity is left unattended, "then, after desire has conceived, it gives birth to sin; and sin, when it is full grown, gives birth to death." In other words, before you know it, something that starts out as tiny as a roach eventually will end the size of an elephant. Do you have friends who will not invite you to certain events? My wife and I experience this a lot. Quite frankly, it is a compliment to your Christian walk. Even though your Christian friends love you, the feeling is that you will put a damper on their party. When their drinking, smoking, and letting their hair down makes them uncomfortable around you, it's obvious that the light in you clashes with the darkness in them.

They (carnal Christians) want to practice carnal Christianity without feeling the presence of the Holy Spirit. What a conundrum.

The Holy Spirit feels quenched (1 Thessalonians 5:19Amplified Bible (AMP)[19] Do not quench (suppress or subdue) the [Holy] Spirit;) and blasphemed when carnal Christians practice carnal Christianity, and carnal Christians feel quenched or grieved when true Christians are in their party space. Just recently, my buddy and I were confronted by this on the golf course. When my friend's walk with Christ became more intense, his profanity ceased, and those who played with him would also minimize or cease their foul language. However, the last time we played, the Christ in us was so strong that the other guys began to curse regularly and completely disregard their previous progress. This let us to believe that the Christ in us created such an agitation within them that it produced a cry for help disguised by profanity. **In other** words, they are primed for salvation.

Lasciviousness
Mark 7:22King James Version (KJV)
[22] Thefts, covetousness, wickedness, deceit, lasciviousness, an evil eye, blasphemy, pride, foolishness:

Lasciviousness refers to the practice of debauchery, lewdness, or licentiousness (lack of moral discipline, especially in sexual conduct; disregard for accepted rules/standards). In a word, to be lascivious is to be lustful. Lasciviousness, used six times only in the New Testament, comes from the Greek word "aselgeia." Lasciviousness was condemned not only by Jesus but also by Jude and the apostles Peter and Paul. Interestingly, the word "lasciviousness" is not used in the more modern Bible translations, but it is found in the older versions such as the American Standard Version, The Young's Literal Translation, and the KJV.

How does the world distinguish between us and them? Why should lost souls practice or convert to Christianity when we look and act more like their lifestyle than they do?

My son went on a date with a presumed woman of God. They met at a public saloon. The day before the meeting, she shared with my son that she couldn't meet that day because she had to go to evening prayer.

On their date, she had a drink and suggested they leave so they could get intimate. My son replied, "What happened to the young lady who went to prayer last night?" Her response: "I left her home." My son was confused and amazed. He was hoping for a woman of virtue and integrity but met the face of carnal Christianity.

On another occasion, he was treated to a strip club in downtown Atlanta. While there frolicking, he was approached by a church member who knew his dad (yours truly). He made a snide comment to him, saying, "Hey, Reverend Washington's son, watch your behavior." What he was trying to say was, "Your dad is a reverend; what are you doing here?" My son politely responded, "I'm not a real Christian but you are, "what are you doing in a strip club"? "You're here sinning, and I'm here sinning, so what makes us different?"

This is a classic example of carnal Christianity as an acceptable lifestyle. However, the point is that it should not be acceptable. Mentoring through prayer is the application to be used to overturn these carnal Christian lifestyle practices.

Example prayer for eradicating carnal Christianity:

Father, in the name of Jesus, we know as long as we are in this flesh, we will fight against fleshly and carnal inclinations, proclivities, and predispositions. But Father, as your son was crucified, please, with all sincerity, crucify, annihilate, abolish, exterminate, obliterate, and expunge the carnal desires and appetites of our pastors, leaders, and ourselves. We desire more than anything to have as our covering pastors and leaders who choose holiness, righteousness, and truth as their daily footstool. Continue to make them men and women after your heart. We pray for the Davidic anointing, the Aaronic anointing, and the Levitical anointing to saturate their hearts, minds, and souls. Any cracks in their clay vessels seal with your Holy Spirit adhesive. In Jesus's name, amen.

Ten

HUMPTY-DUMPTY SYNDROME

2 Timothy 3:1–6: "But know this, that in the last days perilous times will come: For men will be **_lovers of themselves_**, **_lovers of money_**, boasters, proud, blasphemers, disobedient to parents, unthankful, unholy, unloving, unforgiving, slanderers, without self-control, brutal, despisers of good, traitors, headstrong, haughty, lovers of pleasure rather than lovers of God, having a form of godliness but denying its power. And from such people turn away! For of this sort are those who creep into households and make captives of gullible women loaded down with sins, led away by various lusts."

Being on top of the spiritual-leadership food chain, ordained as established generals in the faith, is an assignment that involves great, great responsibility and accountability.

Two scriptures always penetrated my core being while in Bible college: James 3:1 ("My brethren, let not many of you become teachers, knowing that we shall receive a stricter judgment.") and Luke 12:48 ("But he who did not know, yet committed things deserving of stripes, shall be beaten with few. For everyone to whom much is given, from him much will be required; and to whom much has been committed, of him they will ask the more.")

The "stricter judgment" and "much will be required" concepts have kept many generals-in-waiting on the bench or completely out of the game.

The road to the top is always easier than the road to the bottom. "Falling from grace" is the vernacular we use in the kingdom of God. It all began with Satan, who, being the chief musician or the only musician in heaven, decided that his highly revered status wasn't enough. So he set on a course of action that would fulfill his role in the Bible.

Ezekiel 28:11–19 discusses Satan's fall from grace in a grand manner. What I'm discussing here is what all or most leaders in Christ struggle with on a daily basis. What am I referring to—stealing or robbing God's glory? Let me be specifically clear: I'm not saying this; God himself says it in Isaiah.

Isaiah 42:8: "I am the Lord, that is my name; and my glory I will not give to another, nor my praise to carved images."

Isaiah 48:11: "I will rescue you for my sake—yes, for my own sake! I will not let my reputation be tarnished, and I will not share my glory with idols!"

The emphasis in this chapter is how we as men and women of God subtly find ourselves (as humans in the flesh) trying to squeeze in on **God's coveted spotlight**. We give God the glory, teach and preach about giving God the glory, and then find ourselves, ever so slightly puffed up, thinking that it's us—our glory.

Philippians 2:3 (KJV): "Let nothing be done through strife or vainglory [excessive vanity]; but in lowliness of mind let each esteem other better than themselves."

The result of the Humpty Dumpty Syndrome: loss of ministry, loss of family, character defamed, church split, children attacked, testimony canceled, and God's glory faded to black. All of these transgressions produce an unhealthy church.

I've learned that unless a pastor has a <u>prophetic guard</u>,* surrounding them, interceding and mentoring through prayer, being at the top of the food chain can induce a type of hypoxia (altitude sickness). Hypoxia is the sickness Satan suffered from.

Being and staying at the top requires complete, steadfast focus on God. After every wilderness experience follows a mountaintop experience, and after every mountaintop experience follows a wilderness experience.

Mexican boxers have the greatest stamina of all the world boxers. Why? Because of their high-level, high-altitude training. It's all about the breathing at the top.

The Greek word for spirit is "pneuma," which is the same word for "breath" and "air." The higher one goes, the more air/breath/spirit that person needs.

Triathlon training is required just as much for kingdom leaders as it is for Olympians. Focusing on breathing, stamina, the Holy Spirit, and discipline is a course of study not always taught in our institutions of higher learning.

God himself usually teaches this personal discipline; only God himself can teach us how to be self-governed. Now, what the world does teach is "balance." This balance is a false balance that promotes self-aggrandizement.

* Price, Dr. Paula A. 2001, 2008. The Prophet's Handbook: A Guide To Prophecy and Its Operation. Whitaker House (pg. 148)

Proverbs 11:1: "A false balance and unrighteous dealings are extremely offensive and shamefully sinful to the Lord, but a just weight is his delight."

Matthew 4:1–11 (NKJV): "Then Jesus was led up by the Spirit into the wilderness to be tempted by the devil after forty days and forty nights, he was hungry. Now when the tempter came to him, he said, 'If you are the son of God, command that these stones become bread.' But he answered and said, 'It is written, "Man shall not live by bread alone, but by every word that proceeds from the mouth of God."' Then the devil took him up into the holy city, set him on the pinnacle of the temple, and said to him, 'If you are the son of God, throw yourself down. For it is written: "He shall give his angels charge over you," and "in their hands they shall bear you up, lest you dash your foot against a stone."' Jesus said to him, 'It is written again, "You shall not tempt the Lord your God."'

"Again, the devil took him up on an exceedingly high mountain, and showed him all the kingdoms of the world and their glory. And he said to him, 'All these things I will give you if you will fall down and worship me.'

Then Jesus said to him, 'Away with you, Satan! For it is written, "You shall worship the Lord your God, and him only you shall serve."' Then the devil left him, and behold, angels came and ministered to him."

The difference between Jesus in this passage and us is that, number one, he endured the required training for forty days in the wilderness (fasting and prayer). He also received the Holy Spirit. This was his triathlon training. We, on the other hand, hate the wilderness, and fasting is a profane word in our mind-set. Prayer for us is many times not a priority but a burden when in need.

All of this may take a while to sink in. However, like any application, it must be read and reread until results are accomplished.

Remember, this book is an app as well as a book, and with all apps there must be instructions and insight.

We must identify the problem before we can attack the problem.

With the twelve transgressions, I will give scenarios and backdrops to show what the face of each transgression looks like. The conclusion will show how we are to mentor through prayer in a way that will diffuse, derail, and cast down every high thing that exalts itself against the knowledge of God.

2 Corinthians 10:5–6: "Casting down arguments and every high thing that exalts itself against the knowledge of God, bringing every thought into captivity to the obedience of Christ, and being ready to punish all disobedience when your obedience is fulfilled."

What is a high thing: an aspiration or claim to a certain status? Anything that is a high thing (in your mind and thoughts) always takes away from God's glory and puts the glory on yourself.

What does the face of the Humpty-Dumpty syndrome look like?

It's likened to a hot-air balloon that sails or ascends to great heights. The balloon receives a puncture, takes a never-ending fall, and spirals downward to an unfortunate crash. Ask Satan. There was a story in the news recently where two young ladies were parasailing on a very, very windy day. The cable of their sail snapped and carried them broadside into a high-rise building, incurring major injuries. This is also what the face of the Humpty-Dumpty syndrome looks like. One minute you're soaring, and the next minute all hell breaks loose. It could have been prevented if someone had paid attention to the forecast, listened to the Holy Spirit, or had an army of Nathans, a "prophetic guard" praying for them on a 24-7 basis. "Prophetic Guard is a term used in The Prophets Handbook, written by Dr. Paula A. Price, its meaning is; "having a force of seasoned prophets that create the shield of defense that keeps the church clean, pure, focused, and out of Satan's reach." When there aren't enough seasoned Prophets then having an Army of intercessors, to create a shield of defense, would be appropriate and applicable.

Read 2 Samuel 12:1–15.

I believe intercession and intercessors are not only taken for granted but also underutilized in the church. Prayer and intercession (they are the same but different) are the backbone of the church and should be the pillars of the church. You always hear more about Jesus slipping off to pray and interceding than you do about him sitting down to eat. What am I saying? Yes, we make eating more of a priority than praying.

When our spiritual leaders are covered in prayer, mentored through prayer, and surrounded by intercessors for the purpose of focusing on God's glory (the Creator not the creation), then their tenure as God's generals will increase in longevity with minimum cuts, bruises, and backlash.

Sometimes God has to dethrone the men and women of God who have been placed on a pedestal by themselves and their sheep. They become gods (note the lowercase g).

Intercession Defined

Jeremiah 27:18 [18] But if they *are* prophets, and if the word of the Lord is with them, let them now <u>make intercession</u> to the Lord of hosts, that the vessels which are left in the house of the Lord, *in* the house of the king of Judah, and at Jerusalem, do not go to Babylon.'

"Paga" is a Hebrew word meaning to reach, to meet/meet up with someone, or to pressure or urge someone strongly. Paga refers to the extent to which a tribal boundary is reached. Sometimes the verb refers to "falling upon" someone in battle—that is, to meet up with the enemy with hostile intent (1 Kings 2:29). Paga is also translated "make intercession," the idea being that a supplicant catches up with a superior and reaches him with an urgent request. Thus intercession involves reaching God, meeting God, and entreating him for favor.

The word "intercession" has been highly under rated and watered down.

The above definition gives an in-depth understanding of intercession. It is a militaristic term not to be taken for granted or treated lightly.

Ministry is war. When approached with God's perspective, it involves taking back that which rightly belongs to God: souls being held captive by the kingdom of darkness. We represent the Prince of Peace at war with the Prince of Darkness. This is not a game like Battleship or Stratego, played in the sixties, or even today's video games; this is a life-and-death battle that can only be won in the spirit realm.

A new song by Ty Tribbet says, "I got my mind stayed on you." That sentiment is easy to sing but hard to practice.

Sometimes God has to dethrone the men and women of God who have been placed on a pedestal, by themselves and by their sheep. They become gods (lowercase g).

Example prayer for intercession:

Father, we pray in the name of Jesus for your mercy, grace, and truth to be upon us as we pray. Father, we pray for a revolutionary, supernatural move of God to overwhelm our pastors and leaders as you performed on the Damascus road with your servant Paul. Let the supernatural dethroning of their egos begin. We pray for the power of God to increase in them, producing such a decreasing of them that only the Son of God will be seen and heard. Father, we also pray that unlike Saul, who refused to destroy all of the Amelikites, our pastors and leaders will make a concerted daily effort to obliterate all the spiritual and carnal Amelikites in their lives. We pray also that only the sweet aroma of God would emanate from their very being. In Jesus's name, amen.

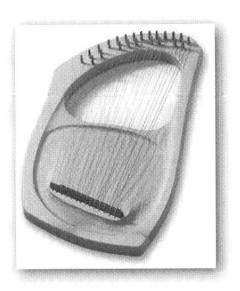

Eleven

Financial Fatigue

*M*any people, especially in churches, are suffering from financial fatigue. I derived this term from a very close friend who experienced this subject firsthand. OK, buckle up for this ride. It's painful but extremely needed. This pink elephant in the room causes not only unhealthy churches but also the demise of many churches. Many times, when performing the autopsy (after the crime has been committed), financial fatigue is rarely if ever discussed. Yes, the church cannot survive nor exist without tithes and offerings; however, there are times when the supply and demand—the input and output—do not reach or meet an equitable distribution. As one pastor so jests, "We have more month than money."

What takes place is this inevitable fatigue.

Offering after offering after offering after offering. Guilt trip after guilt trip after guilt trip. Condemnation after condemnation after condemnation after condemnation.

By now you've gotten my drift. Now here's the kicker: If the Holy Spirit & God the Father are involved, present, in the midst of, and in charge of every project, plan, construction, and vision, the fleecing (defrauding) and shearing of the sheep will not be a burden but a blessing.

Yes, I said shearing (as in shearing of the fleece, if you will). We are sheep, and we are clothed in a woolly covering known as a fleece (soft wooly covering). Once a year the fleece is sheared for the purpose of producing the material used to pay the bills of the church. We call them tithes and offerings. The problem is that in many cases, the sheep are sheared over and over, before they can produce more wool. So the natural order of producing wool is disrupted, and the inevitable results are financial fatigue. You can't get wool from a naked sheep. So what you end up with are disgruntled goats.

When one applies the spiritual stethoscope to the fatigued body, the following symptoms will be always identified: spiritual lethargy, apathy, and dullness; slumber; stupor; sloth; coma; heaviness; weariness; faintness; and burnout. However, identifying them is only the first course of action. Healing these maladies is the next proper course of action. Mentoring through prayer will force the pastor/leadership into a place of around the clock ambulatory prayer.

I'm a firm believer (and will go toe-to-toe with anyone) in the motivation, inspiration, and unctioning of the Holy Spirit concerning matters of giving.

I've sat in services (especially in the African American church) when the Bible was used as a "weapon of pocketbook/wallet/checkbook mass destruction (WPWCMD)". Sheep are often stretched to the absolute limit, especially when their bills take a backseat to the needs of the church. This topic will be extremely unpopular upon reading, and will have many calling me outside of my Christian name. The good news is many will obtain freedom from this application.

THEME OFFERINGS

Every year churches associate the new-year with a New Year's theme and tie it to the offering. On New Year's Eve, I've been a part of the many themed giving services; for example, for 2013, some themes were "God is saying give $2, 013," or "Give $213," or "Give $13 every Sunday for thirteen Sundays." Yes, I even gave, but it was not based on the Holy Spirit's leading; it was based on a spirit of condemnation. The bottom line is that the Holy Spirit's job is to move or unction us to a place of giving. We oftentimes assign the Holy Spirit to the backseat or the unemployment line. My wife and I were used by God to help build a ministry from the ground up with two lovely young pastors. Within the first four years, not one message on tithes and offerings was preached. The church grew and prospered. Was the spirit and purpose of giving taught in new members' classes? Yes! Should there be tithing messages, offering messages, sowing messages, and prosperity messages? Absolutely yes! However, they don't have to be pounded into the sheep if the Holy Spirit is present and allowed to do his job. When he (the Holy Spirit) is not present, financial fatigue will cripple the sheep and the church.

Mentoring through prayer will press the leadership into not only allowing the Holy Spirit to work but also allowing a series of day of Pentecost services where the people can be filled with the power and presence of the Holy Spirit. Let's be honest: If the people are not filled by the indwelling power of the Holy Spirit, the evidence will be lacking. OK, here is where many theologies will be rattled. Yes when you receive the gift of salvation, you receive God's spirit. However, God himself decrees and declares in Acts 1:8 that there is an infilling accompanied by power that one receives that is separate from receiving God's spirit at salvation. This infilling proves itself via evidence. I believe and have experienced this initial evidence to be speaking in tongues. There are many wannabe theologians who would dispute this fact. However, spending too much time on this subject would take away from the purpose of mentoring through prayer.

There's a book entitled Riding in the Second Chariot (author K. Edward Copeland) that teaches leaders and ministers how to ride alongside the pastor. What's absent in many of our pastors is their inability to ride alongside the Holy Spirit. Several years ago I had a vision (in a sleep state, if you will) of a portrait/painting depicting a family pulling up to a church and gazing at the church billboard out front that said, "Holy Spirit in Charge; Pastor No Longer Needed." Now this statement is guaranteed to ruffle lots of feathers.

Don't get angry with me. In Christendom, this is the unhealthy state many of our churches are in.

Of course the pastor is still needed; however, when the pastor is unyielding to the Holy Spirit, the service is flesh driven. When the pastor yields to the Holy Spirit, the service is Holy Spirit driven. The ultimate purpose of this book is to unequivocally sound the alarm that the Holy Spirit must be in charge. When the Holy Spirit is in charge and the people are filled with the Holy Spirit, giving will be Holy Spirit driven. When it is not, the people and the church are hurt and affected, all leading to collapse and implosion.

Example prayer for financial fatigue:

Father, we know that one of your greatest priorities is for your church on earth to represent the bride you desire. A beautiful bride, a bride in waiting, a prosperous bride. A well-groomed bride, a financially sound bride. A bride who represents sound judgment and honorable stewardship. And Father, as we know these truths to be evident, our prayer is that your spirit the Holy Spirit would be completely in charge. In charge of our giving and in charge of our pastors and leaders and their decision making. Father, be in charge of our tithes, offerings, spiritual gifts, lending, and borrowing. And Father, always remind us that everything belongs to you and not to us. In Jesus Name Amen

Twelve

❖❖❖

PULPIT MISUSE, MISAPPROPRIATION, AND ABUSE

Victory is <u>not</u> won in the pulpit by firing intellectual bullets or wise-cracks but in the prayer closet. It is won or lost before the preacher even steps into the pulpit.

Too many times the pastor uses the pulpit to air out in-house laundry, attack indifferences that took place behind the scenes, and/or highlight vanity/egomaniacal carnality. The pulpit is a microcosm of the Holy of Holies. The pulpit is sacred and should be revered.

Exodus 28:33–35 says, "And upon its hem you shall make pomegranates of blue, purple, and scarlet, all around its hem, and bells of gold between them all around: a golden bell and a pomegranate, a golden bell and a pomegranate, upon the hem of the robe all around. And it shall be upon Aaron when he ministers, and its sound will be heard when he goes into the holy place before the Lord and when he comes out, that he may not die."

For twenty-three years, I've been in the pews for hundreds of services and sermons. My first pastor truly taught me the dos and don'ts of ministry. I heard not only open rebukes but also church laundry aired from the pulpit. One of the don'ts was, and is, making personal (unnamed) attacks because you (the leader) felt attacked.

69

Many times a pastors or leader's character or veracity is attacked by a disgruntled sheep, and the rebuke (expression of sharp disapproval or criticism), was laced in and through the message/sermon. In smaller congregations the majority of congregants knew who the focus of the rebuke was directed toward. In a larger congregation or mega-church, the pastor would consider it a teachable moment. Sometimes it's about the person and not the point. At the point of rebuke or presumed admonishment, the ego/flesh has taken over, and the spirit man has taken a backseat. Let's say it this way: the flesh increases while the spirit decreases. Anytime flesh is involved, the people shut down, and God's glory fades to black. God's pulpit is always intended to bring him glory, not to vent over the sheep's venting and voicing of their opinion outside of the sanctuary. I've learned that once this takes place in the beginning of the message, the people shut down, and whatever was preached or taught was never heard nor received.

Another pulpit faux pas is the self-aggrandizement of accumulated blessings, body parts (physical attributes) and ability to teach and preach the gospel. (Self-aggrandizement is an act undertaken to increase your own power and influence or to draw attention to your own importance ego trip, self-aggrandizement.) The congregation knows how blessed you are; that's why they are there. One does not have to flaunt what one is blessed with in the face of the people Sunday after Sunday. Mentoring through prayer will, when prayed effectively and specifically, push the pastor/leader to allow the Holy Spirit's conviction, pushing the pastor/leader into a place of self-examination. This will reroute, if you will, his or her thinking to a focused, stay-on-message teaching and preaching.

The church is not ours, the sheep are not ours, the gifts are not ours, and the sacred office is not ours. They all belong to Christ. If some of the things we say from the pulpit now were said during the Levitical priesthood times, the bells would sound off, and the priest would not make it out of the Holy of Holies. Death would be their ultimate demise.

The problem is that we don't have the fear of the Lord described in the book of Exodus, Proverbs, and the book of Psalms.

Proverbs 9:10: "The fear of the Lord is the beginning of wisdom, and the knowledge of the Holy One is understanding."

Psalm 128:1–2: "Blessed is everyone who fears the Lord, who walks in his ways. When you eat the labor of your hands, you shall be happy, and it shall be well with you." Much of what we retort (: to pay or hurl back : return) from the pulpit is not sound wisdom or sound doctrine. Wisdom from Holy Spirit would prevent us from hurtful and senseless diatribes: (a bitter and abusive speech or piece of writing). Ninety-nine percent of our diatribes should be handled in closed-door meetings, not publicly in front of the congregation. As you can see, the words "diatribe" and "retort" define and identify this transgression perfectly.

Yes, the Word does tell us in Hebrews 4:12 (NKJV), "For the word of God is living and powerful, and sharper than any two-edged sword, piercing even to the division of soul and spirit, and of joints and marrow, and is a discerner of the thoughts and intents of the heart."

However, the Word is the Word, and personal attack is personal attack. The pulpit is to be used to disseminate the Word of God to edify, to build up and not tear down. Is this a slow arduous process? Yes, but you will see the results nonetheless.

"The pulpit must never ever be used as a weapon to wage a personal attack against a member of the church". The Pulpit should never be used as a weapon of mass destruction!!!!

Flesh and ego must be addressed with intense mentoring through prayer.

Personal attacks from the pastor are a direct result of **distressing spirits** (tormenting depression) I repeat **Distressing Spirits** that have overwhelmed him or her. That's when the harp/lyre must be played, to hopefully remove the distressing spirit.

Example prayer for pulpit misuse:

Father, we pray in the name of Jesus that the wisdom of God, the knowledge of God, the understanding of God, the character of God, the righteousness of God, and the holiness of God would permeate, saturate, and overwhelm our pastors/leaders in such a way that inappropriate behavior, comments, and unsound doctrine would not be an option nor a consideration. Each time they enter the pulpit on behalf of a Holy God, arrest them in the spirit to make pulpit misuse, abuse, and misappropriation be utterly impossible. And Father if, and when these acts occur, chasten them as only you can to further make them acceptable use for the Master's glory. We pray this prayer according to 2 Timothy 2:19–21. In Jesus's name, amen.

Thirteen

Fear of the Supernatural Christ Anointing

Preaching without anointing/unction kills instead of giving life. The Word does not live unless the anointing/unction is upon the preacher. Isaiah 10:27 says, "It shall come to pass in that day that his burden will be taken away from your shoulder, and his yoke from your neck, and the yoke will be destroyed because of the anointing oil." Preaching, teaching, praying, healing, without power and anointing is basically an act in futility.

The anointing of God and the power of God are essential in today's church and the kingdom of God on earth. Luke 19:9–10 says that when Jesus was Zacchaeus, he said to him, "Today salvation has come to this house, because this man, too, is a son of Abraham. For the Son of Man came to seek and to save the lost."

The name of the anointing that empowers Christ's ministers for their service to the Lord is chrio. As an aspect of the Lord's many anointing's, this one is distinct in that it may also be called the ministry power anointing. Chrio describes the outpouring of the Holy Spirit that specifically rests on his officers and ministers in active service. Chrio furnishes what is needed to perform the duties and exploits of one's call. According to Strong's Concordance, the word "chrio" is used four times in the New Testament. Only one of those times is it applied outside of Christ, which is not to say that it does not apply to human ministers, because that is inaccurate. What it is to say, though, it is that the chrio anointing specifically empowers divine service. The single time the word "chrio" is used for anointing for human ministers is in 2 Corinthians 1:21 in relation to the apostles. All this states that the chrio anointing to minister is more than the chrisma all believers get. It goes along with Acts 1:8, where the Lord instructs his followers to remain in Jerusalem until they are endued (filled) with power from on high in Luke 24:49. Otherwise, it is only used in the New Testament one other time.

Without chrio, ministers rely entirely on their human talents and have a lesser degree of potency and consequently less ministry success. Chrio is a power anointing, period. It comes upon the Lord's servants for one reason and one reason only: to empower them as effective witnesses of God's Word, truth, and power. Because of this goal, chrio also supplies what it takes to yield to the moves and waves of the Holy Spirit. Without it, Christ's ministers cannot quite submit to God's will, be used by his power, or execute what cannot ordinarily be done by mortal humans. The anointing, when manifested in this context, uses the vessel rather than the normal course of affairs where the vessel uses the anointing in ministry.[3]

The supernatural Christ anointing destroys yokes, chains, shackles, strongholds, wrong mind-sets, and religious boxes.

The supernatural Christ anointing is the engine that drives the car, the rudder that steers the ship, and the able in our ability. Without it we are mere mortals; with it we become supernatural beings on earth.

Isaiah 10:27 says, "It shall come to pass in that day that his burden will be taken away from your shoulder and his yoke from your neck, and the yoke will be destroyed because of the anointing oil."

1 John 2:27 (AMP) says, "But as for you, the anointing the sacred appointment, the unction that you received from him abides permanently in you; so then you have no need that anyone should instruct you. But just as his anointing teaches you concerning everything and is true and is no

---

3 Price, Dr. Paula A. 1994. The Five-Fold Ministry Offices, *Ephesians 4:11-12*. Flaming Vision Publication (pg. 61)

falsehood, so you must abide in live in, never depart from him being rooted in him, knit to him, just as his anointing has taught you to do."

The supernatural Christ anointing of God should be present in teaching, preaching, counseling, pasturing, shepherding, children's and youth ministry, laying on of hands, and marriage counseling.

The book of Acts is one of our greatest examples of the supernatural Christ anointing in action. Throughout the book of Acts, we see the anointing and the unction of God being manifested through the apostles.

- Acts 5:15: Peter is so filled with the Holy Spirit that even his shadow has the power to heal, a fact that makes Groundhog Day even less impressive.
- Acts 9:36–42: Peter raises Tabitha from the dead. Almost as impressive is that Tabitha was also named Dorcas. I think it's clear why she went by Tabitha.
- Acts 20:9–12: A young man named Eutychus falls asleep and falls to his death out a third-story window in the middle of preaching. Paul later brings him back to life.
- Acts 28:3–6: A poisonous viper sprang out of a campfire and latched onto Paul's arm, only to be thrust off with Paul suffering no harm. The witnesses then thought Paul was a god.

In addition to all of these, apostles witnessed healing the blind (9:17–18), the paralyzed (9:33–35), the lame (14:7–9), the possessed (16:16–18), and even a man with severe diarrhea (28:7–8). You see, the Bible has everything!

Acts of the Apostles also has three dramatic jailbreaks (5:17–25; 12:5–11; 16:25–30), divinely inspired pyrotechnics at Pentecost (2:2–6), healing relics (19:11–12) and a worship service so powerful that the earth quakes (4:31)!

All of these acts and manifestations are attributed to the supernatural Christ anointing on the lives of the apostles, the Christ (Anointed One) in the apostles and the power of God manifested through the apostles.

Are we seeing these manifestations today as we saw them then? No! Because the anointing is being used for the purpose of entertainment and the tickling of ears. The anointing is being used as a "magical pixie dust" to lull the saints/sheep into an entertainment stupor. We are so inoculated with the desire to be entertained that our senses are dulled. God commissions Isaiah in chapter 6 to tell the people concerning their senses, how they've become dulled.

Isaiah 6:8–11

Then I heard the voice of the Lord saying, "Whom shall I send? And who will go for us?" And I said, "Here am I. Send me!" He said, "Go and tell this people: 'Be ever hearing, but never understanding; be ever seeing, but never perceiving.' Make the heart of this people calloused; make their ears dull and close their eyes. Otherwise they might see with their eyes, hear with their ears, Understand with their hearts, and turn and be healed." Then I said, "For how long, Lord?"

Yes, there are anointed men and women of God, with the supernatural Christ anointing on and in their lives. However, the gifts of God are without repentance (Romans 11:29). God gives us his gifts through his son, Jesus the Christ, and he doesn't take them back. This does not mean that his gifts and his anointing are to be bastardized and marketed like the snake-oil salesman hawking elixir at the carnival. The Gifts are to be used for healing and deliverance for those who are oppressed and depressed.

We see the example of false imitations and perpetration (carrying out as a crime or deception) of the anointing in Acts 19:13–16, with the sons of Sceva. While trying to cast out evil spirits, the evil spirits not only mocked the sons of Sceva, but they also jumped on them and beat them silly. The opposite causes the evil spirits to recognize who you are and bow down under the supernatural Christ anointing (Mark 5).

Example prayer for combating fear of anointing:

Father, we pray in the name of Jesus for your glory to be revealed concerning your anointing as it was revealed in the book of Acts.

We pray that wherever your supernatural Christ anointing is, you will be there also. We pray that whenever you're anointing and gifts are used for anything other than to glorify you that your chastening will be in effect. Empower your ministers, officers, and leaders with the true supernatural Christ anointing that will open blind eyes, heal diseases, cause limbs to grow, and allow those with mental and physical paralysis to walk. Father, if you did it before with your apostles, you can do it again. Holy Spirit, bring forth conviction where conviction is needed, and that conviction will produce repentance. Please, Father, let your supernatural Christ anointing be used for its intended purpose in Isaiah 61.

Isaiah 61 (AMP)

The spirit of the Lord God is upon me, because the Lord has anointed and qualified me to preach the gospel of good tidings to the meek, the poor, and afflicted; he has sent me to bind up and heal the brokenhearted, to proclaim liberty to the [physical and spiritual] captives and the opening of the prison and of the eyes to those who are bound,

To proclaim the acceptable year of the Lord [the year of his favor] and the day of vengeance of our God, to comfort all who mourn, to grant [consolation and joy] to those who mourn in Zion—to give them an ornament (a garland or diadem) of beauty instead of ashes, the oil of joy instead of mourning, the garment [expressive] of praise instead of a heavy, burdened, and failing spirit—that they may be called oaks of righteousness [lofty, strong, and magnificent, distinguished for uprightness, justice, and right standing with God], the planting of the Lord, that he may be glorified.

Fourteen

FIVEFOLD-OFFICE ANNIHILATION

Hosea 4:6: "The people perish (are destroyed) because of a lack of knowledge."

We fear the unknown, so we hide rather than explore. The pastor, teacher, and evangelist have long been accepted as leaders in the church. The prophet and the apostle, on the other hand, have been dismissed and dispatched to a spiritual abyss, as mentioned in the earlier chapter (chapter 7).

The church will always operate outside of <u>God's divine order</u> if and when the fivefold officers and ministry are not in operation. The pastor, teacher, and evangelist are the preeminent, premier officers almost always on post in the church. In the fifties, sixties, and seventies, the pastor and the teacher were the only officers on post, with the women relegated to Sunday school, nursery, and kitchen duties. I won't delve into the female role in the church at this time but rather reserve it for my next book.

Not only do the churches fear the unknown (the prophet and the apostle are considered the unknown), but they also fear the uncovering and the unveiling that the prophet and apostle bring.

Prophetic's in general are feared because of a lack of teaching. We also fear Team Ministry. We hoard the gifts and the office.

It's not like we are completely unfamiliar with the office of the prophet; prophets exist throughout the Old and New Testaments. We even study (in Bible institutions of higher learning) the major and minor prophets of the Bible. The body of Christ must embrace the unknown; it's where God resides. Faith is the substance of things hoped for and the evidence of things not seen (Hebrews 11:1). Evidence of things not seen is the operative statement in this scripture.

The unknown relates to things that are unseen, incomprehensible, out of the ordinary, out of the box, behind the scenes, behind the curtain, and beneath the surface.

Colossians 1:24–29 speaks of the hidden things of God being revealed to the saints of God.

There is a fear with some pastors in some churches that by exploring, accepting, receiving, and allowing the restoration and rehabilitation of the apostle and the prophet, we take the risk of receiving and allowing false prophets and apostles in our ministries. In Matthew 23:34, the Word informs us that "God will send us prophets and wise men." In Matthew 24:11, "God informs that there will also be false prophets who will arise and mislead us. Although they will arise with power (counterfeit power), they will not and cannot stop the advancement of God's provision of divine order in the church."

Let's liken this phenomenon to the removal of physical education from the school curriculum. What you have when that happens is a society of obese children who become obese adults. The collateral damage creates a broken health-care system and a nation of people with multiple illnesses, particularly high blood pressure and diabetes. What I'm saying is that the absence of the *complete* fivefold ministry *produces incompleteness*, *divine disorder*, and *incurable maladies*; saints have stunted growth or are immature saints, gifts go untapped, and the people of God never reach their full potential in God. However, I do not intend on making this chapter a microcosmic book on the fivefold ministry; there are enough books written that discuss the offices in detail.

I'm writing this chapter to sound the alarm on the rooftops to do my part in restoring, rehabilitating, and advancing the fivefold offices.

Let's take a moment and look at the obvious intentions of God, revealed in Ephesians 4:7–13 of the Message Bible:

> But that doesn't mean you should all look and speak and act the same. Out of the generosity of Christ, each of us is given his own gift. The text for this is,
> He climbed the high mountain,
> He captured the enemy and seized the booty,
> He handed it all out in gifts to the people.

Is it not true that the one who climbed up also climbed down, down to the valley of earth? And the one who climbed down is the one who climbed back up, up to highest heaven. He handed out gifts above and below—filled heaven and earth with his gifts. He handed out gifts of apostle, prophet, evangelist, and pastor-teacher to train Christ's followers in skilled servant work, working within Christ's body, the church, until we're all moving rhythmically and easily with each other, efficient and graceful in response to God's son, fully mature adults, fully developed within and without, fully alive like Christ.

God's message here is maturity, growing up in the way he intended for us to grow. If God ordained five officers to train his body, why are we intent on utilizing one, two, or three? My first pastor and Teacher, Dr. Paula A. Price (whom I referenced in the last chapter from her book on the fivefold ministry), taught me the intimate understanding of each officer. This is so lacking in our churches/ministries today. She taught us that there should be one vessel per office in order to produce maximum efficiency. This doesn't mean that there are not apostles (although rare) who can operate in all five offices. The point is that we handicap ourselves when we handicap the Holy Spirit's work to bring forth divine order in our churches/ministries.

Again, let's look at the obvious need. A surgeon practices surgery because of his countless hours of study to become a surgeon. A lawyer litigates trials with efficiency because of his countless numbers of hours in law school to become a lawyer. A contractor builds homes because of his laborious skills and insight on construction. A pilot flies jets because of his countless flying hours. We wouldn't want or ask a lawyer to perform intricate surgery, and we wouldn't want a surgeon to litigate a lawsuit for us. So why should it be any different in the kingdom of God?

So often we have prophets trying to pastors, or evangelists trying to be prophets. The fact that a person has a gift of prophesy does not make him or her a prophet. Because a teacher can deliver a great word does not make him or her a pastor. I could go on and on, but it would defeat the short-term goal of this chapter. Its goal is to incite a provocative discussion around every boardroom table, with the hopes of eliminating the fear of not only the prophet and apostle but of the fivefold ministry in general.

Are you afraid? Is your pastor or leader afraid? I pray that you have been challenged and you will challenge your leadership. Just think, you may be a prophet hiding out in the pews of <u>purgatory</u>; the pastor may see your gift but afraid to call it into existence. Or you may be afraid to speak up for fear of rejection. "God did not call us to a spirit of fear but of power, love, and a sound mind." (2 Timothy 1:7 NKJV).

Example prayer for upholding the fivefold ministry:

Father, in the name of Jesus, we first want to repent for our collective ignorance concerning the fivefold ministry offices and officers. We pray in the name of Jesus for the veil of darkness over the eyes of our pastors, ministers, and leaders concerning the fivefold gifts to be removed forever. We pray for those officers (unbeknownst) to their leaders, sitting in the pews dying, to be educated, taught, and discipled for your glory. We pray for your Word in Ephesians to be rightly divided so your body will line up with you and be in divine order. Most of all,

Lord, we pray for the spirit of fear to be obliterated and abolished concerning these matters. Father, restore and revive the prophet and the apostle to their rightful place. In Jesus's name, amen.

Fifteen

SPIRITUAL GIFTS BENEDICTION

One of the greatest injustices in the church is the inability of pastors to *identify* (ascertain, recognize, pinpoint, connect) the sheep among them and the gifts in those sheep. Very few pastors have this gift. Yes, this identification is extremely difficult and challenging. However, it can and has been done with those who spend hours and hours in the face and presence of God.

I know, because I'm a product of a pastor who identified the gifts and calling on my life.

Yes, we take new-member classes and take the spiritual gifts test. However, sadly enough, it ends with the class, and we are shuffled in the church-volunteer/worker category (e.g., usher, greeter, teacher, deacon, elder, etc.).

Sadly, *needs* (outer needs- if you will) of the church are fulfilled in this scenario, but *innate* (internal gifts, given at birth born in the spirit) gifts, talents, and callings are never realized or tapped into. Just recently, a visiting pastor admitted angrily, that one of his members left the church to pursue the gift/office of the prophet and a deeper understanding of Prophetic's. The pastor told the member in so many words, "I'm not equipped in that area," so it's OK to leave.

Most pastors will never admit to being ill equipped in the spiritual gifts area, especially Prophetic's. Mentoring through prayer will create an atmosphere where gifts can be birthed, and the pastor's keen sense of discernment will and can be enhanced.

The most overlooked benefit in our spiritual gifts benefits package is speaking in tongues and the interpretation of tongues. We have seen a plethora of what can be interpreted as voodoo practices of speaking in tongues. What am I saying? Thousands of church services (especially in the fifties, sixties, seventies, eighties, and nineties) throughout the body of Christ believed that a circus display and implementation (if you will) of receiving the gift of speaking in tongues were considered normal. Apostle Paul fought with this and tried to bring clarity and normalcy through his teachings. The bottom line is we need Tongues and Interpretation.

To list the peculiar displays and manifestations would be too numerous. However, to say what was really the Holy Spirit and what wasn't would place me in the theater of theological interpretation like the theological forefathers, who wrote volumes and volumes of canonical reviews without being filled by the indwelling Holy Spirit.

In other words, all scripture is inspired by God (2 Timothy 3:16) All Scripture is God-breathed and is useful for teaching, rebuking, correcting and training in righteousness) and all theology is inspired by man's interpretation of God, without the Holy Spirit.

Yes, I said it and will stand by it. Why? Because I personally know the person, persona, and the personality of the Holy Spirit. He leads me, guides me, and teaches me all truth. Does he give me an advantage? Yes. Many times, I would like to say it's an unfair advantage. However, there were many great men and women of God, such as Billy Graham, who have admitted to having never spoke in tongues. Foaming at the mouth, people being injured, and a host of other uncontrollable occurrences would be considered a practice in carnality. On the other hand there was a tremendous outpouring of the Holy Spirit in Florida and Toronto. Below is an excerpt from Wikipedia:

> *The Brownsville Revival (also known as the Pensacola Outpouring) was a widely reported religious phenomenon that began within the Pentecostal movement on Father's Day, June 18, 1995, at Brownsville Assembly of God in Pensacola, Florida. Characteristics of the Brownsville Revival movement, as with other Christian religious revivals, included acts of repentance by parishioners and a call to holiness, said to be inspired by the manifestation of the Holy Spirit. Some of the occurrences in this revival fit the description of moments of religious ecstasy. More than four million people are reported to have attended the meetings from its beginnings in 1995 to around 2000.

I would like to focus on the phrase "religious ecstasy." In Florida and in Toronto, Christians were seen laughing in an uncontrollable manner; supernatural healings occurred, and mouths/teeth were even filled with gold. Was this God in a grand manner? Yes, I believe it was. Does God operate in a grand manner? Absolutely yes. It's chronicled all throughout the Bible.

The crazy thing is that there are many skeptics who to this day are still trying to disprove the awesome powers of God then and the awesome power of God now. The Holy Spirit is a gentleman. When he operates, we should see it as his brilliant manifestations and not with a spirit of confusion or bewilderment.

*Brownsville Revival
From Wikipedia, the free encyclopedia

Yes, there can be bewilderment. Don't get me wrong; as in the parting of the Red Sea and God's providing manna from heaven, these signs and wonders appear bewildering to the natural mind. However, this bewilderment comes with a divine purpose. Every act and manifestation of the Holy Spirit should have a divine manifestation and purpose. God is not the author of confusion.

1 Corinthians 14:33: "For God is not the author of confusion but of peace, as in all the churches of the saints."

We began this chapter with the Title "Spiritual Gifts Benediction," which means that because of the lack of teaching and the fearful expectation of disorder and confusion, we pronounce the spiritual gifts dead on arrival (DOA).

The apostle Paul spent several chapters teaching and discussing the spiritual gifts especially speaking in tongues.

1 Corinthians 14:5: "I wish you all spoke with tongues, but even more that you prophesied; for he who prophesies is greater than he who speaks with tongues, unless indeed he interprets, that the church may receive edification."

However, it is obvious that in Paul's dissertation, he had a certain fearful expectation and anticipation that disorder and confusion would be evident. After all, the indwelling of the Holy Spirit was new to the body, and exercising the gifts would not only take practice, but also a referee, for continued education and explanation.

The idea of spiritual gifts is synonymous to going higher. The indwelling and the infilling of the Holy Spirit allows the benefits of the Holy Spirit to be activated within those who are not afraid to ask. Fear on behalf of the leadership, as well as the congregants/sheep, is the number-one roadblock to every Christian's growth and development. Being afraid of heights (going to a higher level in God) is the second-largest roadblock.

SPIITUAL-ALTITUDE SICKNESS

Hypoxia is a term used when discussing altitude sickness (also mentioned in the chapter on the Humpty-Dumpty syndrome).

The literal definition of hypoxia (also known as hypoxiation) is a condition in which the body or a region of the body is deprived of adequate oxygen supply.

The reason why it's worth revisiting is because, going too another level requires going higher. Going higher means that one must be filled by the Holy Spirit. Spirit is the same word (as previously mentioned) for breath and air. The higher one goes, the more Holy Spirit/air/breath one needs. The supernatural realm is where spirit operates, and where we must operate, to obtain more of God—more revelation, more wisdom, more knowledge, more of God's hidden mystery, and most of all more power.

I remember praying in the spirit as a young Christian for ten and fifteen minutes at a time. The longer and stronger I prayed, the higher I would go. There were times that I would pray so long and hard that the level of heights (in the supernatural) to which God would take me would literally scare me. Christians don't have a problem flying in airplanes, but they do have a problem flying with God to supernatural realms and atmospheres. It may seem like I have veered off a bit, but this teaching all ties into the topic of spiritual gifts benediction. You see fear—fear of heights in particular—is and has prevented us from taking hold of our "spiritual gifts benefits package". If every Christian (and I mean every) operated with power in at least one spiritual gift, the kingdom of God on earth would be far more advanced in our quest to <u>win souls</u> for his kingdom. That is what be a soldier for Christ is all about isn't it?

This app of mentoring through prayer, when applied with power, will do the following:

- Help eliminate fear concerning the receivership of the Holy Spirit.
- Dispel the myths surrounding the Holy Spirit's operation in our lives (especially   in revealing the Holy Spirit as a person and not a thing).

- Create an atmosphere of divine order.
- **Build an Army of "Mentoring Through Prayer" Intercessors.**

What that means is that when we pray for our pastors and leaders, to not only operate in the gifts, but also teach their congregation the importance of operating in the gifts, the desire for the gifts will be increased and received.

Many congregants have received the gift of the Holy Spirit, however, when attending a church that doesn't operate in the gifts, or does so only partially, the gifts lie dormant so that the benediction/last rights might as well be pronounced.

Not until an activation, reactivation, and impartation by the leadership/pastor will we begin to see a full assault on the kingdom of darkness through our operation in the gifts. Mentoring through prayer will accomplish this through the nudging, pushing, petitioning, supplicating, and pressing of God to move our leaders/pastors in the direction of spiritual gifts.

Romans 1:11–12: "For I long to see you, that I may impart to you some spiritual gift, so that you may be established (fix, strengthen)—that is, that I may be encouraged together with you by the mutual faith both of you and me."

There are four identifiable reasons why Christians shy away from (intentionally & unintentionally) the indwelling and infilling Holy Spirit:

1. Fear of the unknown (2 Timothy 1:7)
2. Accountability (convicts us of sin John 16:8)
3. Lack of knowledge (Hosea 4:6)
4. Fear of heights (hypoxia) (Ephesians 3:16-19 Amp)

We fear what we don't know and what we don't understand. Hosea 4:6a, b: "My people are destroyed for lack of knowledge; because you the priestly nation have rejected knowledge, I will also reject you that you shall be no priest to me."

The lack of understanding of God's sheep is mostly attributed to the pastors or leadership's inability and/or reluctance to teach the people. After the impartation, there must be education. The age old dispute over the initial evidence (speaking in tongues) of the indwelling/infilling has placed us in a spiritual bondage and spiritual lethargy.

I'm reminded of the movie AVP: Alien vs. Predator, where the alien was locked up (chained) deep underground for a number of years. When foreigners showed up, they accidentally set off the mysterious puzzle. The puzzle set in motion, the activation and release, of the mother of all aliens. The key word here is activation. Once there is a indwelling and an infilling of the Holy Spirit, it must be activated.

To be filled with the Holy Spirit is to be energized and controlled by the third person of the Godhead in such a way that under the acknowledged lordship of Jesus Christ, the full presence and power of God are experienced. Spirit-filling leads to renewal, obedience, boldness in testimony, and an arresting quality in believers' lives and most of all receives power.

Acts 1:8: "But you shall receive power when the Holy Spirit has come upon you; and you shall be witnesses to me in Jerusalem, and in all Judea and Samaria, and to the end of the earth."

You see, the entire purpose of receiving the baptism of the Holy Spirit is the endowment of power.

The spiritual gifts chart that follows will give all who read this book great insight into the gifts of God.

Spiritual Gift	Definition	Scriptural Reference	Distinctive	Traits
Administration	The God given ability to understand what makes an organization function, and the special ability to plan and execute procedures that accomplish the goals of the ministry	1Cor. 12:28 Acts 6:1-7 Ex. 18:13-26	-Develop strategies or plans to reach identified goals. -organize people, tasks, or events. -Assist ministries to become more effective and efficient.	-Thorough -Objective -Responsible -Organized -Goal-oriented -Efficient -Conscientious
DISCERNMENT	The God given ability to distinguish between truth and error, good and evil, right and wrong.	1Cor. 12:10, Acts 5:1-4, Rom. 9:1	-Identity deception in others with accuracy and appropriateness -Are able to sense the presence of evil. -Recognize inconsistencies in teaching or message.	-Perceptive -Insightful -Sensitive -Intuitive -Truthful -Decisive
ENCOURAGE-MENT	God-given ability to present words of comfort, consolation, and encouragement, so to strengthen, or urge to action, those who are discouraged or wavering in their faith.	Rom. 12:8; Acts 11:22-24; Acts 15:30-32	-Comfort others to trust and hope in the promises of God. -Motivate others to grow. -Urge others to action by applying biblical truth.	-Positive -Motivating -Affirming -Reassuring -Supportive -Trustworthy

Spiritual Gift	Definition	Scriptural Reference	Distinctive	Traits
Evangelism	The God given ability to effectively communicate the gospel to unbelievers so they respond in faith and move toward discipleship.	Eph. 4:11; Acts 8:5-6; Acts 14:21	-Communicate the message of Christ with clarity and conviction. -Seek out opportunities to talk to unbelievers to faith in Christ.	-Sincere -Candid -Influential -Confident -Commitment-Oriented
FAITH	The God- given ability to act on God's promises with confidence and unwavering belief in God' ability to fulfill His purposes.	1Cor. 12:9; 1Cor. 13:2; Rom. 4:19-21	-Act in complete confidence of God's ability to overcome obstacles. -Advance the cause of Christ because they go forward when others will not. -Ask God for what is needed and trust Him for His provision.	-Prayerful -optimistic -trusting -assured -inspiring -Hopeful -positive
GIVING	The God-given ability to contribute money and resources to the work of The Lord with cheerfulness and liberality.	Rom. 12:8; 2 Cor. 6:8; Luke 21:1-4	-Manage their finances and limit their lifestyle in order to give as much of their resources as possible. -meet tangible needs that enable spiritual growth to occur. -support the work of the ministry with sacrificial gifts to advance the Kingdom.	-Responsible -Stewardship-oriented -resourceful -charitable -disciplined

Spiritual Gift	Definition	Scriptural Reference	Distinctive	Traits
HELPS	The God-given ability to accomplish practical and necessary, behind the scenes tasks, which free up, support, and meet the needs of others.	1 Cor. 12:28; Rom 12:7; Acts 9:36; Rom. 16:1-2	-serve behind the scenes wherever needed. -see the tangible and practical things to be done and enjoy doing them. Attach spiritual value to practical service.	-Available -willing -Reliable -loyal -dependable -whatever-it-takes attitude
Hospitality	The God-given ability to care for people by providing fellowship, food, and lodging.	1Peter 4:9-10, Rom. 12:13, Luke 10:38	-Provide an ENVIRONMENT where people feel valued and cared for. -seek ways to context people together into meaningful relationships. -set people at ease in unfamiliar surroundings.	-Friendly -gracious -inviting -caring -responsive -warm
Intercession	The gift of intercession is the God-given ability to consistently pray on behalf of and for others, seeing frequent specific results.	Rom. 8:26-27; Col. 4:12-13	-Feel compelled to earnestly pray on behalf of someone or some cause. -Have a daily awareness of the spiritual battles being waged and commit to pray. -pray in response to the leading of the Spirit, Whether they understand it or not.	-Advocate -sincere -trustworthy -burden-bearer -Spiritually sensitive

Spiritual Gift	Definition	Scriptural Reference	Distinctive	Traits
PROPHECY	The God-given ability to reveal God's truth and proclaim it in a timely and relevant manner for understanding, correction, repentance, or edification.	Rom. 12.6; 1 Cor. 12:10,28, 1 Cor. 13:2	-See a truth that others often fail to see and challenge them to respond. -Understand God's heart and mind through experiences He takes them through. -Expose sin or deception in others for the purpose of reconciliation.	-Discerning -Compelling -Uncompromising -Outspoken -Authoritative -Confronting -Convicting
SHEPHERDING	The God-given ability to assume long term personal responsibility for the spiritual welfare of a group of believers by nurturing and guiding them toward ongoing spiritual maturity.	Eph. 4:11-12, 1 Peter 5:1-4; 1Tim. 3:-13	-Provide guidance and oversight to a group of God's people. -Establish trust and confidence through long-term relationships. -Lead and protect those within their span of care.	-Nurturing -Guiding -Protective -Supportive -Relational -Influencing

Spiritual Gift	Definition	Scriptural Reference	Distinctive	Traits
TEACHING	The God-given ability to understand, clearly explain, and apply the Word of God in such a way that it is clearly understood by others.	Rom. 12:7; 1 Cor. 12:28-29; Acts 18:24:-28	-Give attention to detail and accuracy. -Prepare through extended times of study and reflection. -Challenge listeners simply and practically with the truths of scriptures.	-Disciplined -Perceptive -Teachable -Authoritative -Practical -Analytical -Articulate
WISDOM	THE GOD GIVEN ABILITY TO APPLY SPIRITUAL TRUTH EFFECTIVELY TO MEET A NEED IN A SPECIFIC SITUATION	1 Cor. 12:8; James 3:13-18; 1 Cor. 2:3-5; Prov. 1:20	-Focus on the unseen consequences in determining the next steps to take -Provide God-given solutions in the midst of conflict and confusion. Apply spiritual truth in specific and practical ways.	-Sensible -Insightful -Practical -Wise -Fair -Experienced
TONGUES SPEAKING	Tongues (speaking) - The special ability God gives to some to speak prayer or praise in a language they have never learned or to communicate a message from God to His people. The special ability God gives to some to speak in a language not previously learned so unbelievers can		- may receive a spontaneous message from God which is made known to His body through the gift of interpretation - communicate a message given by God for the church (if there is someone to interpret) - speak in a language they have never learned and do not understand - worship the Lord with unknown words	-FAITH -YIELDING -INTERCESSION

Spiritual Gift	Definition	Scriptural Reference	Distinctive	Traits
	hear God's message in their own language		too deep for the mind to comprehend - experience an intimacy with God which inspires them to serve and edify others - speak in tongues as a private prayer language - When used in a group setting, an interpretation must take place, or else the one speaking the tongue should remain silent.	

Spiritual Gift	Definition	Scriptural Reference	Distinctive	Traits
TONGUES INTERPRETAION	Tongues (interpreting) - The special ability God gives to some translate the message of one who speaks in tongues. If a tongue is spoken without an interpretation, the speaker is edified If the tongue is interpreted, it is for the edification of the body.		- express with an interpretation a word by the Spirit which edifies the Body - enable the gift of tongues to build up the church by interpreting God's message for the people.	-OBEDIENCE
HEALING	Healing (Sign Gift) - The special ability God gives to some to serve as a human instrument through whom it pleases Him to cure illness and restore health (physically, emotionally, mentally, or spiritually) apart from the use of natural means.	1 Corinthians 12:7-11 1 Corinthians 12:28-31 Acts 3:1-10 Acts 14:8-10 James 5:14-16 Luke 9:1-2	People with this gift: - demonstrate the power of God - bring restoration to the sick and diseased - authenticate a message from God through healing - use it as an opportunity to communicate a Biblical truth and to see God glorified - pray, touch, or speak words that miraculously bring healing to one's body.	The divine enablement to be God's means for restoring people to wholeness

98

Spiritual Gift	Definition	Scriptural Reference	Distinctive	Traits
MIRACLES	Miracles (Sign Gift) - The special ability God gives to some to serve as a human intermediary through whom He pleases to perform acts of supernatural power that are recognized by others to have altered the ordinary course of nature and authenticated the divine commission.	1 Corinthians 12:7 11 1 Corinthians 12:28-31 Mark 16:17-18 Acts 9:36-42 Acts 20:9-12 Hebrews 2:4 Romans 15:17-19 Acts 8:13 Acts 19:11-12	-speak God's truth and may have it authenticated by an accompanying miracle - express confidence in God's faithfulness and ability to manifest Christ's presence - bring the ministry and message of Jesus Christ with power - claim God to be the source of miracles and glorify the Lord - represent Christ and through this gift, point people to a relationship with Christ.	

Example prayer for spiritual gifts—benediction:

Father, we (the yet unborn) pray with great tenacity and truth for every church, cathedral, synagogue, worship center, and mosque to immediately be turned into a maternity ward, where the Holy Spirit can give birth to every gift that is yet unborn and lying dormant.

Father, we hear the cries of the sheep in labor pains yearning to be a part of your Word manifested in the New Testament scriptures. Father, please open the eyes of the ministers and leaders who themselves do not have the gift of discernment. With this discernment, enable them to identify the gifts in the sheep you have entrusted them with. Father, we loose (release) your Word in the book of Joel, in the book of Ephesians, and in Corinthians, that identify your gifts. Father, expedite these prayers immediately for your glory. Set those being held hostage to religion and tradition in our churches free. In Jesus's name, amen.

Sixteen

CHURCH-MEMBERSHIP RECIDIVISM

"Recidivism" is a tendency to relapse into a previous condition or mode of behavior. For some, this term is usually used in the substance-abuse cycle or the criminal-history cycle.

However, I have chosen to use this phrase to identify the constant turnover of church membership. There are many members who stick around for the long haul. However, there are many members/congregants who come and go with unspeakable regularity. What's ironic is that all of the other eleven transgressions contribute to the ongoing membership-recidivism dilemma.

Pastors and leaders have been trying to figure out for centuries why they have a difficult time keeping members.

Now all they have to do is read this book or use this application.

One of my best-known sheep-maintenance experiences was in an Assembly of God church in New Jersey. When a first-time visitor would attend the church, the very next day, a staff member would give that person a call and/or a visit. Immediately, the church would inquire as to what the person's needs were and how the church could meet those needs. This, my friends, is the ultimate outreach technique. Many times our outreach/evangelism efforts hone in on reaching those who have not visited the church. Our efforts should be honed in on both with the priority of how do we maintain those God has already sent to us.

Example Prayer to Prevent Church-Membership Recidivism

Father, in the Name of Jesus, we ask You to divinely intervene on behalf of the potential members who walk through the doors of every church each Sunday. It is Your desire to Seek and save the Lost as stated in Luke 19:10 "For the Son of Man came to seek and to save the lost." Father please also intercede on behalf of our leaders who are unaware of the proper way to receive and maintain new sheep. In Jesus Name Amen.

Seventeen

SALVATION DEPRIVATION

Through much research, I've concluded that some denominations (not all) have resigned to multiple altar calls or multiple calls to the altar. For example, church membership (open the doors of the church), church covering, rededication, special prayer for healing/deliverance from sickness/disease, and, last but not least, salvation. Salvation has taken a backseat to church membership. Yes, membership is important, but it should never overshadow salvation. Now, not all denominations practice this process/procedure. Some denominations do not have altar calls at all. Unfortunately, I have to use the dreaded word "denomination." This unfortunate term (meaning a recognized autonomous branch of the Christian church) has become a curse in the body of Christ. No, there will not be denominations in heaven.

The end result of denominationalism is salvation deprivation. The opposite of denominationalism is uniformity. Each denomination approaches salvation or the call to salvation in a different manner. I believe this causes and produces confusion. What does confusion produce? Souls being deprived of salvation, and there is a vacuum in our need to receive/announce/invite souls to receive Christ and enter into the kingdom of God.

When evangelist Billy Graham finishes preaching, his infamous invitation to receive Christ always draws thousands to the altar. Graham only spoke of church membership after salvation was ministered and sealed. And his message concerning church membership was that one should find a local church that preached the unadulterated Word of God and where salvation was the priority, not an agenda item.

If the people get saved in a particular church (at the altar, during the altar call, or even during the message), they ultimately will be led by the Spirit to join a church; more than likely, it will be the church they were saved at. Mentoring through prayer will move, if not eliminate, this travesty. What's the real travesty? In some denominations/churches (I reiterate, some not all), we have five or more separate altar calls.

The salvation altar call gets lost, muddled, displaced, and confusing. Heaven knows that if I (a seasoned saint) am confused, those coming to the altar for the first time ever have to be somewhat disoriented.

An altar-friendly church is what God has established for us to come boldly before his throne of grace. From Genesis to Revelation, God lays out his plan of salvation.

Diminishing the call to salvation versus the call to church membership (and other invitations) performs an incredible injustice to the soul who desires to be saved.

Deprivation is the act or process of removing something usually essential for mental or physical well-being, or the condition resulting from that removal. Related words include "shortage," "scarcity," and "insufficiency."

When there is an insufficiency of salvation and its message, a scarcity of salvation and its message, and a shortage of salvation and its message, we ultimately end up with salvation deprivation.

Matthew 28:16–20 says, "Then the eleven disciples went away into Galilee, to the mountain that Jesus had appointed for them. When they saw him, they worshiped him; but some doubted. And Jesus came and spoke to them, saying, 'All authority has been given to me in heaven and on earth. Go therefore and make disciples of all the nations, baptizing them in the name of the Father and of the Son and of the Holy Spirit, teaching them to observe all things that I have commanded you; and lo, I am with you always, even to the end of the age.'" Amen. It is very important to include verses 16 and 17 because of two very crucial words: "worshiped" and "doubted."

After Jesus rose from the grave—the greatest out-of-the-box miracle ever known to mankind—two things happened (and still happen today): Those who believed were saved and bowed down and worshipped God the Son, and those who did not believe doubted. Belief with the heart produces salvation (2 Corinthians 5:17 below). The world is still baffled by this great feat; author Hugh Schonfield has written books to try to disprove it: *Those Incredible Christians* and *The Passover Plot*.

Doubt produces salvation deprivation.

Mark 16:15–16 (AMP): "And he said to them, 'Go into all the world and preach and publish openly the good news the gospel to every creature of the whole human race. He who believes and who adheres to and trusts in and relies on the gospel and him whom it sets forth and is baptized will be saved from the penalty of eternal death; but he who does not believe (doubts) and who does not adhere to and trust in and rely on the gospel and him whom it sets forth will be condemned.'"

2 Corinthians 5:17: "Therefore if any person is engrafted in Christ the Messiah, he is a new creation a new creature altogether; the old previous moral and spiritual condition has passed away. Behold, the fresh and new has come!"

2 Corinthians 5:17 (NKJV): "Therefore, if anyone is in Christ, he is a new creation; old things have passed away; behold, all things have become new."

Example prayer for avoiding salvation deprivation:

Father, we pray specifically, that the above passages would be highly activated, unlocked, implemented, manifested, and applied to our leaders first and then to the souls you have ordained to be saved. Father, we repent for ourselves and our leaders who have not made salvation a priority at every service and Bible study. Please forgive us of these travesties, injustices, and oversights. Now, Father, with all of your power and might, divinely and supernaturally touch your/our leaders and ministers to be complete and made whole—to be effective in the ministry of salvation. And Father, whatever you have to do to crucify our flesh and their flesh to make us meet for your (the Master's) use, do expeditiously so that not another soul may be lost. In Jesus's omnipotent name, amen.

2 Timothy 2:19–21 (AMP): "But the firm foundation of (laid by) God stands, sure and unshaken, bearing this seal (inscription): The Lord knows those who are his, and let everyone who names himself by the name of the Lord give up all iniquity and stand aloof from it. But in a great house there are not only vessels of gold and silver, but also utensils of wood and earthenware, and some for honorable and noble use and some for menial and ignoble use. So whoever cleanses himself from what is ignoble and unclean, who separates himself from contact with contaminating and corrupting influences will then himself be a vessel set apart and useful for honorable and noble purposes, consecrated and profitable to the Master, fit and ready for any good work."

2 Timothy 2:19–21 (NLT): "But God's truth stands firm like a foundation stone with this inscription: 'The Lord knows those who are his,' and 'All who belong to the Lord must turn away from evil.' In a wealthy home some utensils are made of gold and silver, and some are made of wood and clay. The expensive utensils are used for special occasions, and the cheap ones are for everyday use. If you keep yourself pure, you will be a special utensil for honorable use. Your life will be clean, and you will be ready for the Master to use you for every good work."

About the Author

Rev. Craig G. Washington is a graduate of the Everlasting Life Bible Institute. He has served as a church builder and planter, a marriage and family counselor, and a substance abuse counselor during his twenty-five years of ministry. He currently lives in Kennesaw, Georgia, with his wife of nineteen years. He has two adult sons.

Dedication

I dedicate this Book to God and my Wife. My Wife because she has endured great trials and tribulations with longsuffering, love and grace. God because He has preserved my life and wrote this book through me. For that I'm grateful.

Contact Information:

Rev. Craig G. Washington

609-516-7205 craigval55@gmail.com Call or email for speaking engagements

Made in the USA
Charleston, SC
01 June 2015